a pocket

RHY

imagination for a new generation

2006 Poetry Competition for 7-11 year-olds

GW00504269

Eastern England Vol II

Edited by Young Writers

Editorial Team

Lynsey Hawkins
Allison Dowse
Claire Tupholme
Donna Samworth
Aimée Vanstone
Gemma Hearn
Angela Fairbrace
Heather Killingray
Jessica Woodbridge

 Young**Writers**

First published in Great Britain in 2006 by:
Young Writers
Remus House
Coltsfoot Drive
Peterborough
PE2 9JX
Telephone: 01733 890066
Website: www.youngwriters.co.uk

SB ISBN 1 84602 448 X

Foreword

Young Writers was established in 1991 and has been passionately devoted to the promotion of reading and writing in children and young adults ever since. The quest continues today. Young Writers remains as committed to the nurturing of poetic and literary talent as ever.

This year's Young Writers competition has proven as vibrant and dynamic as ever and we are delighted to present a showcase of the best poetry from across the UK and in some cases overseas. Each poem has been selected from a wealth of *A Pocketful Of Rhyme* entries before ultimately being published in this, our fourteenth primary school poetry series.

Once again, we have been supremely impressed by the overall quality of the entries we have received. The imagination, energy and creativity which has gone into each young writer's entry made choosing the poems a challenging and often difficult but ultimately hugely rewarding task - the general high standard of the work submitted ensured this opportunity to bring their poetry to a larger appreciative audience.

We sincerely hope you are pleased with this final collection and that you will enjoy *A Pocketful Of Rhyme Eastern England Vol II* for many years to come.

Contents

Katie McDermott (7)	17
Bradley Harris (7)	17
Caroline Quinn (8)	17
Michael Catlin (8)	18
Archie Wishart (8)	18
Holly Bishop (8)	18
Leon Hart (8)	18
Nicholas Faulkner (7)	19
Ross Taylor (7)	19
Leon Liasis (7)	19
James Ansell (8)	19
Canev Mehmet (7)	20
Natasha (8)	20
Robert Jones (7)	20
Ross Payne (7)	21
T J Bruce-Coker (8)	21
Erin Stack (7)	21
Abita Nanthakumar (11)	22
Russell Price (7)	22
Ronak Ross (7)	22
Afagh Mulazadeh (8)	23
Jake Langley Burns (7)	23
Lucy Carter (7)	23
Max Berlevy (7)	23
Micaela Opoku-Mensah (10)	24
Pauline Ellinas (10)	24
Georgia Chandler (8)	24
Dijon Richmond-Gaisie (11)	24
Sophie Moreton (11)	25
Donovan Murfet (11)	25
Jake Nixon (11)	26
Mark Taylor (10)	26
Nick Adamou (11)	27
Oren David (10)	27
Andrea Panayi (11)	27
Claudia Sarjant (11)	28
Claudia Dixon (10)	28
Peter Michael (11)	29
Leah Kline (10)	29
Jamie Leanne Ibbott (7)	29
Holly Tyler (11)	30
Marwan Warda (11)	30

Bradley Sayers (10)   30
James Nesbitt (10)   31
Amy Pettitt (10)   31
Rebecca Perris (11)   32

Dewhurst St Mary Primary School, Cheshunt
Ben Hopkins (9)   32
Samuel Harris (8)   32
Grace Wheeler (11)   33
Matt Simmons (11)   33
Harry Smith (10)   34
Katharine Keen (10)   34
Christine Parkins (10)   35
Max Newell (11)   35
Lia Mardling (10)   36
Jessica Stevenson (10)   36
Charlie Prosser (10)   36
Jaimal Baxter (8)   37
Joshua Cliss (8)   37
Charlie Murphy (8)   38
Georgia Harrison (8)   38
Charlotte Franklin (10)   39
Kitty Newell (9)   39
Alice Hornett (10)   40
Ben Mitchell (8)   40
Travis Parker (8)   41
Holly Turner (9)   41
George White (8)   41
Joe Saul-Baylis (8)   42
Stacey Maunders (9)   42
Rebecca Evans (9)   42
Tommy Hunn (8)   43
Emelia Montanari (9)   44
Lauren Burton (9)   44
Fuat Ahmet (9)   45
Leah Fisher (9)   45
Joseph Pinkney (10)   46
Luke Aspland (9)   46
Shelby Fraser (10)   47
Reuben Gatens (8)   47
Emily Phillips (10)   48

Matthew Ball (8)	48
Abbie Ward (9)	49
Vanessa Coomes (8)	49
Taylor Jermy (9)	50
Glenn Miller (8)	50
Jamie Bain (10)	51
Liam O'Leary (10)	51
Aimee Bracebridge (11)	52
Chas Flynn (9)	52
Kate Charlton (10)	52
Freddie Stevenson (8)	53
Ria Graham (9)	53
Cody T Chamberlain (8)	54
Abi Fisher (8)	55
Nicole Mcliveney (8)	56
Jack Morter (11)	57
Alisha Buckle & Jessica Morrell (11)	58
Elena Pelech (10)	58
Rachel Howes (10)	59
Sam Chaney (10)	59
Warwick Byrne (9)	60
Chelsea Helmond-Jones (9)	60
Paige Burgess (8)	61
Kerris Mezen (9)	61
Lauren Taylor (10)	62
Elizabeth Easterbrook (10)	62
Jamie Thomas (10)	63

Fairhaven CE (VA) Primary School, South Walsham

Josh Rimmer (10)	63
Audie Warren (11)	64
William Ives (10)	64
Jessica Futter (11)	65
Emma Rose (10)	65
James Starkings (9)	66
Claire Edwards (10)	66
Shannon Mills (9)	67
Katherine Lund (10)	67
Michael Cole (11)	68
Robert Lee (10)	68
Katy Cooper (9)	69

Natasha Church (10)	69
Steven Freer (11)	70
James Hodgson (10)	70
Sean Blyth (10)	71
Jac Hudson (10)	71
Tom Goodrum (10)	72

Ferrars Junior School, Luton

Perry McNally (10)	72
Lee Thorne (10)	73
Iffra Rashid (10)	73
Kyle Dwyer (10)	73
Timothy Mutton (11)	74
Jade Wakelin (11)	74
Jahny'e Knight (11)	75
Zhane Kilby (10)	75
Sarah Dempsey (9)	76
Raees Khan (11)	76
Andrew Brooks (10)	77
Christopher Gray (11)	77
Mohammed Nabeel Asghar (10)	78
Monica Mangoro (10)	78
Rhys Davies (11)	79
Nadia Ahmed (10)	79
Laura Colclough (11)	79
Tristan Owen (11)	80
Olivia Popoola (10)	80
Victoria Adkins (10)	80
Selva Ross (11)	81
Grace Burch (10)	81
Kier Buot (11)	81
Lucy Mardell (10)	82
Jeremy Aytoun (12)	82
Rachel Brown (10)	82
Sarah Owen (8)	83
Arandeep Bains (11)	83
Joshua Hedley (11)	83
Muhammed Haque (10)	84
Hayley Fuller (10)	84
Jade Richards & Mollie Macdonald (8)	85
Hanifa Tidjani (9)	86

Emmanuel Gooding (9)	86
Mark Lomax (10)	87
Chloe Moore (10)	87

Flamstead End Primary School, Cheshunt

Lauren Wood (8)	87
Harry Goodwin (8)	88
Amy Littleford (8)	88
Rachel Banner (8)	89
Georginana Ioannou (8)	89
Alex Kiely (8)	90
Ben Parker (8)	90
Alfie Merridale (8)	91
Vanessa Blair (8)	91
Samuel Rowden (8)	91
Daniel Key (8)	92
Melissa Howard (9)	92
Raynor Belloguet (9)	93
Brandon Fagan (9)	93
Kelsey Barron (9)	94
India Wayland (9)	94
Courtney Chidgzey (8)	95
Benn Lee (9)	95
Amelia Diston (9)	96
Joe Hannigan (9)	96
Brandon Joy (8)	97
Lucy Carter-Vale (8)	97
Lara Gamby (8)	98
Sarah Winter	98
Rebecca Dawson (9)	99
Jack Rowden (8)	99
Chloe Richards (8)	100
Harry Richardson (8)	100
Jay Barlow (8)	100
Aaron Elliott (9)	101
Benjamin Howell (9)	101

Gaddesden Row JMI School, Hemel Hempstead

Erin Thackeray (7)	102
Aylwen Hadley (8)	103

Lucy Hodson (8)   104
Conor Grant (8)   105

Garden Fields JMI School, St Albans
Jamie Henderson (9)   106
Chrystal Smith (8)   106
Louise Anstee (11)   107
Joanne Anstee (8)   107
Pritish Chauhan (11)   108
Rosalind Bennett (8)   109
Lauren Hart & Freya McCann (9)   109
Vikesh Chauhan (8)   110

Gresham's Preparatory School, Holt
Grace Pitkethly (9)   111
Layla Myers (9)   112
Alice Hare (9)   113
Jack Barter (10)   114
Clare Mawson (9)   115
Gregor Bailey (9)   116
Karina Olsen (9)   116
Harriet Shaw (8)   117
Caitlin Astley (9)   118
Abbie Glover (9)   119
Florence Baldwin (9)   120
Conrad Redmayne (10)   121

Greyfriars Primary School, King's Lynn
Miranda Skeats (8)   121
Kourtney Hitchcock (10)   122
Kodiey Yallop (11)   122
Sabrina Hichcock (8)   123
Megan Watson (7)   123
Harry Twyman (8)   123
Callum Flynn Wallace (9)   124
Stewart Scott (7)   124
Louis Morrish (8)   124
Elvin Cheung (10)   125
Ryan Lee Reeve (10)   125
Chloe Ellis (9)   125
Jessica Hill (9)   126

Bexley Loose (9)	126
Jamie Hall (10)	126
Lucy Barnes (10)	127
Tadas Frieturminkas (11)	127
Caitlin Nolan (10)	127
Cara Hawes (8)	128
Dylan Goodfellow (9)	128
Thomas Steward (7)	128
Sophie-Louise Nolan (8)	129
Roy Black (8)	129
Harrie Reed (7)	129
Chloe Wigg (8)	130
Ben Austin (9)	130
Jacob Emerson (8)	130
Melissa Skeats (8)	131
Alison Sanpher (8)	131
Ben Wright (8)	131
Christopher Pavey (8)	132
Lauren Gillies (9)	132
Thea Joslin (8)	132
Kyle Rhys Hitchcock (7)	133
Elliot Holland (8)	133

Gunthorpe School, Peterborough

Georgia Kendall (9)	134
Matthew Baldwin (9)	134
Paige Johnston (9)	135
Connor Penson (10)	136
Samantha Setchfield (9)	136
Thomas Croote (9)	137
Jade Rossell (10)	137
Laura Kohter (10)	138
Naomi Amanda Stewart (9)	138

Henham & Ugley Primary School, Henham

Nathan Giles-Donovan (11)	139
Rhiannah Whitelock (10)	140
Rosie Greaves (11)	141
Sally Reeve-Arnold (11)	142
Charlotte Albiston (10)	143
Jessica Hogg (11)	144

Henry Parker (11) — 145
Eloise Robinson (11) — 146
Rosina Brooks (11) — 147
Adam Machin (10) — 148
Gina Martinelli (11) — 149
Benjamin Clark (11) — 150
Michael Jordan (10) — 151

Hexton JMI School, Hitchin

Poppy Allen-Quarmby (11) — 152
Lily Rogerson (8) — 153
Lucy Rosser (10) — 154
Jamie Rose (8) — 154
Jamie White (10) — 155
Max Wolstencroft (8) — 155
Prian Chauhan (10) — 156
Annabel Katie Forde (11) — 156
Ben Lawson (10) — 157
Abigail Gee (8) — 157
Amy Rogerson (9) — 158

Holbrook Primary School, Holbrook

Stuart Hall (8) — 158
Sean Cuddihy (9) — 159
Taylor Handel (8) — 160
Harriet Sawyer (9) — 160
Oliver Sellers (9) — 161
Jordan Goodwin (9) — 161
Samuel Kocurek (8) — 161
Joshua Allday (8) — 162
Paddy Atkinson (9) — 162
George Rennison (8) — 163
Nicole Anscomb (9) — 163
Brooke Ward-Ashton (9) — 164
Eleanor Carey (8) — 164
Phoebe Maunder (9) — 165
Declan Lee (8) — 165

The Poems

The Magic Box
(Based on 'Magic Box' by Kit Wright)

I will put in the box . . .
A tiny salty tear from the moon,
A star that fell a long time ago,
A beautiful red flower that pricked my hand.

I will put in the box . . .
A muddy horseshoe from the track,
A bowl of water that sticks together,
A flute of so many colours and the most amazing sound.

I will put in the box . . .
A cracker of so many surprises,
A sprinkling of glitter from the north,
A piece of gold tooth.

My box is made of orange paper
And different patterned stars.
In my box I go to sleep
And dream of all the things in it.

Georgina Kenny (8)
Chrishall Primary School, Chrishall

The Hail

The hail is like a lion,
Gushing to the ground,
Leaping onto the buildings,
Making a rattly sound,
Bright and hard like pebbles
Falling into the sky,
From high, high, high!
Suddenly it goes quiet and calm,
Resting on its claw,
On the side of his palm.

Jason Emmerson (10)
Danegrove Primary School, East Barnet

The Lightning

The spitting rain grows and grows,
It becomes furious and strong.
Lightning is as mean as a cobra
Spitting its 1,000 volts of venom.

Disintegrating whatever is in its way,
Burning, disintegrating, ashes,
As the sun peeps out,
Lightning declares war! War! War!

Soldier Vs lion in the Roman fort,
Fight till the death!
As terrible as World War II,
Lightning lion and sunny soldier!

Lightning surrenders to mighty sun,
But it will attack again,
With one last spit of electric
Venom it slithers into the sky.

Jamie Gilgan (10)
Danegrove Primary School, East Barnet

The Stunning Waves

From the stunning waves,
The river comes down
From the rocky mountains,
It hits the ground
Hour upon hour,
It races past,
But when the sea is calm
It is shallow,
Glistening from the sun,
Getting light from the sun,
Then its journey is over.

George Jumbo (10)
Danegrove Primary School, East Barnet

A River's Journey

A river's journey is very long,
It twists and twirls elegantly,
Dodging anything crossing its path.

Gently flowing downstream,
A calm nature like a rabbit,
Sun twinkles down on it and sparkles.

As it gets faster, it rapidly picks up speed,
It starts crashing against rocks,
Raging and splashing.

Suddenly it falls down,
Its cold spray scattering everywhere,
Rushing to the bottom it hits the sharp rocks.

Now at the bottom
It spirals itself out wide
And gently flows to the sea.

Now at the sea, it rests
And its waves gallop to the shore like horses!

Becky Carter (11)
Danegrove Primary School, East Barnet

Silver

Silver is like a bear
disguised in the snow.

Silver is like an owl
flying very slow.

Silver is like a wolf
howling through the night.

Silver is like the sun
spreading its rays of light.

Sezer Kukul (10)
Danegrove Primary School, East Barnet

The Wind

The wind is like a whirling, turning snake
Hissing with anger,
Shaking his tail, making lots of noise.
Slithering along the ground,
Hissing and hissing!
Lashing out, catching rats,
Spinning round and round,
Gushing wind through the path,
Rustling up leaves, making them crunch.

When the sun goes down
And the moon comes up,
The snake lies there like a still piece of paper
Thrown into the bin!
In the morning he wakes up with a big yawn
With his mouth open wide,
Ready to start another big day!

Sophie Preston (11)
Danegrove Primary School, East Barnet

The Journey Of A River

Raging down the mountain,
Whooshing like a fountain.
Crashes down the waterfall,
Smash, bash, smash, bash.
Determined to reach the ocean,
Showing such emotion.

Avoiding every boulder,
The night is getting colder.
Roaring through the landscape,
Trying to escape.
The mean, vicious river
Once again is trying to reach the . . .
Deep, deep sea!

Yasmin Nikkhouee (11)
Danegrove Primary School, East Barnet

The River

The river thrashes down banks,
It crashes the rocks angrily,
It is bold but gentle,
It glistens like stars at night,
It's spectacular.
If you get in a river
It slithers round you.
Rivers are frothy like clouds,
They sparkle brightly,
Splashing down the waterfall,
But when the day fades
You can't see the river,
Wait until tomorrow when it begins
Its journey once again.

Christianna Koukoullis (10)
Danegrove Primary School, East Barnet

The Fire

The fire is a ferocious lion
Ready to pounce on its prey.
It looks as cute as a puppy,
Its colours shining brightly.
As it gets bigger and bigger
Its true colours show.
It is like a rogue elephant
Destroying everything in its path
And turning it to ash,
Its destructive flames licking at every tree.
As rain showers from the sky
The fire dies and dies.

Cameron Phillips (11)
Danegrove Primary School, East Barnet

The River

The calm, rippling stream
Starting its winding journey
Down the mountain.
Suddenly hitting a fallen boulder
And sliding into a
Frothing, thrashing, meandering rapid
Lined with jagged rocks.
Then an explosion . . .
The water pours down a
Spectacular waterfall
Into a steamy pool
Of glistening water.
A vast valley lies ahead,
The water races
Down the valley
To meet the deep blue sea
As dawn sets . . .

Amy Kraven (11)
Danegrove Primary School, East Barnet

The River

She twists and turns as she goes up and down,
Colliding over silky rocks and under dark tunnels,
She swishes and sways,
But when she gets angry she ferociously pushes
Through everything and anything in her way.
Strong as a bull, she destroys everything in her sight,
Pulling it apart and ripping it into shreds.
But on calm and peaceful nights she is back to her own bubbly self,
Playful as a puppy, relaxed as a dove.
That is the way she is, cheerful as a fluffy kitten
Playing with a ball of wool.

Jazmin Bhangoo (10)
Danegrove Primary School, East Barnet

The Journey Of A River

The rain falls down from the sky,
On to the peak that's oh so high.
The snow then melts to form a river,
It then trickles down with a slither.
It hits ragged rocks, scattered around,
Way up high and on the ground.
Water droplets flying everywhere,
Frothing up, in the air.
It calms down through the day,
Flowing down the mountain away and away
Crashing down the waterfall raging,
Looking fierce, crashing, bashing and roaring.
It's calming down more and more.
It's twisting and turning to form a stream
And now it's flowed out to join the sea.

Rebecca King (11)
Danegrove Primary School, East Barnet

The Stunning River

The
Stunning
River
Crashes
Down
From
Rocky
Mountains,
It
Dashes
And
Flashes
With
Glistening
Light!

Daniel Reynolds (11)
Danegrove Primary School, East Barnet

The Journey Of A River

The raging, rocky river,
Starting up in the snow-
Tipped mountain.
Crashing angrily into anything
In its path,
Whooshing and whooping,
Making an explosion as it clashes
Into boulders.

The raging rocky river,
Roaring boldly.
The beautiful river frothing,
Meandering at every opportunity,
Swaying spectacularly.

The raging, rocky river,
Racing down to the waterfall.
The furious and vicious river,
So vast it's seen for miles around.

At dusk the sun is reflecting,
On the glistening water.
It's a sight to be seen,
So lovely!

Harshni Chandaria (11)
Danegrove Primary School, East Barnet

Thunder And Lightning

Thunder and lightning
Loud and fast,
Strikes you down
To the ground,
You won't get up
After the ring,
You will not live,
You will not die,
You will be in pain tonight.

Ryan Houldsworth (11)
Danegrove Primary School, East Barnet

Hello I'm Super Silver

I am Super Silver, I am very cool.
I am Super Silver, I am good in school.

I love eating limes
And I'm happy all the time.

I have lots of friends,
I wear a contact lens.

I am hot, I am cold,
I am also very bold.

I am so shiny, that I can make you blind.
I am so shiny, I am easy to find.

I am funny and exciting,
I am as quick as lightning.

I got a big fine,
I go to bed at nine.

See you later, alligator.

Scott Curbishley (7)
Danegrove Primary School, East Barnet

Family Thinks

My mummy thinks it's funny
to have lots of honey.

My daddy thinks it's good
to have lots of wood.

My sister thinks it's great
to have lots of mates.

My brother thinks he's clever
to see the weather.

Lily Stevenson (7)
Danegrove Primary School, East Barnet

A Dog Named Claude

My name is Little Claude
And sometimes I get bored.

When that happens to me,
I get very naughty.

I start to bite people's toes,
Scarves, coats or Babygros.

Everything to make them play,
But all I get is 'Go away'.

So off I trot, back to bed,
Where I can rest my weary head.

Dreams of chicken, walks and bones,
Of this lovely place called home.

Lola Scriven (7)
Danegrove Primary School, East Barnet

The Flying Pea

The bee took my pea,
I caught the bee.
The pea went 'Wheee!'
The bee sat on the pea
And then the bee stung me!

Christian Michael (8)
Danegrove Primary School, East Barnet

Shiver In A River

There once was a man called Shiver
Who jumped in a great big river.
He touched his toes
And blew his nose
And then he started to quiver.

Hannah Linton (7)
Danegrove Primary School, East Barnet

Mr Weather

He dribbles on the clouds
And it falls down as rain.
He sucks it all up
And then he does it all again.

He makes a lot of snow
But he also makes ice.
He likes a lot of things
And is also very nice.

He's got a lot of friends
Who are very kind,
He is the best friend
You could ever find.

He is very strong,
He blows off people's hats!
But he's quite afraid of things
Especially vampire bats.

Jonah Solomons (8)
Danegrove Primary School, East Barnet

Tigers

Lovely tigers orange and black.
They like to eat meat.
After their meat, they go to sleep,
The cubs are very playful.

From different countries,
They are endangered.
They walk gracefully
And they look cuddly.

David Horne (7)
Danegrove Primary School, East Barnet

Miss Sugar

M iss Sugar is so sweet.
I like her little treats.
S he likes everyone in school.
S he has a swimming pool.

S o does a boy called Matt.
U Irika thinks he's fat.
G one he was, one day.
A ngry Miss Sugar made him pay!
R oss got his place.

Dana Rahimi (8)
Danegrove Primary School, East Barnet

Miss Honey Is A Lovely Lady

M iss Honey is a lovely lady.
I n PE we play.
'S hh,' she said.
S he is doing her work.

H oney is her favourite.
O h look it is Miss Honey.
N o arguments with her.
E asy work for me.
Y ey here's Miss Honey.

Amy Horne (7)
Danegrove Primary School, East Barnet

Animal - Spider

S pinning webs on trees,
P laying on the webs.
I n and out of the grass,
D ragging flies into its mouth.
E ggs. 'You found eggs.' 'Oh no!'
R un away!

Oguzhan Tumsa (7)
Danegrove Primary School, East Barnet

Hallowe'en

H ello, trick or treat?
A lways coming to lots of houses to get lots of sweets.
L ast year I got lots of jelly beans to eat.
L ast year you gave me sweets.
O n Hallowe'en you get lots of sweets.
W ith people dressed up in spooky stuff,
E *ek, eek*, it's very scary out here.
E erie and spooky, rats and lots of horrible stuff,
N early at the next house but not yet.

Katie McDermott (7)
Danegrove Primary School, East Barnet

Monster

M y monster is red,
'O nka' is his name.
N ever dies,
S ometimes he is lazy.
T he monster is fat,
E ats all day,
R oars all night.

Bradley Harris (7)
Danegrove Primary School, East Barnet

Angel The Cat

A cat sleeps on my bed.
N ice and fluffy.
G inger he is.
E very day he has a meal,
L oves food so much.

Caroline Quinn (8)
Danegrove Primary School, East Barnet

The Man Who Bought A Train

There once was a man from Spain
Who bought a big red train.
He ran after a toad,
All the way down the road,
And that made him complain.

Michael Catlin (8)
Danegrove Primary School, East Barnet

Jake

There once was a boy called Jake
Who really liked chocolate cake.
He gave the bowl a lick,
Which made him feel sick
And he couldn't eat any more cake.

Archie Wishart (8)
Danegrove Primary School, East Barnet

A Guy From Bry

There once was a guy from Bry
Who ate a huge apple pie,
Then he got sick,
He hit himself with a brick,
Then suddenly he started to cry.

Holly Bishop (8)
Danegrove Primary School, East Barnet

Lions

Lions are orange,
They are a bit lazy and big.
Lions like to eat a lot of meat,
With very big teeth.

Leon Hart (8)
Danegrove Primary School, East Barnet

A Dangerous Shark

S mooth and sneaky
H ard as metal
A ngry and vicious
R uin all the boats and kill the people
K eep away from this dangerous and vile creature.

Nicholas Faulkner (7)
Danegrove Primary School, East Barnet

Tigers

Tigers are sneaky,
They have stripes on their fur.
Tigers are lovely and lazy,
They eat meat.

Ross Taylor (7)
Danegrove Primary School, East Barnet

Lion

L eaping through the forest eating lots of meat,
I mpossible to beat.
O utstanding big feet.
N earby the lion waits for its prey.

Leon Liasis (7)
Danegrove Primary School, East Barnet

Leopards - Haiku

Leopards have black spots
On their long, wide yellow backs
With their speedy legs.

James Ansell (8)
Danegrove Primary School, East Barnet

Big Blue Sea

Shiny as can be,
The children come to see,
White sand, blue sky
In the daytime.
Big blue sea,
Water comes down on me.
In the night, sparkling, twinkling stars.
Big blue sea,
Please don't take my castle away,
With your beautiful wave.

Canev Mehmet (7)
Danegrove Primary School, East Barnet

Roald Dahl

Roald Dahl was a very famous person.
He was kind too.
He was as funny as The Simpsons,
But he was an author too.
He wrote fantastic books,
My favourite is 'Charlie and the Chocolate Factory'.
He was interesting.

Natasha (8)
Danegrove Primary School, East Barnet

Castles

Lots of things go on in a castle,
When a war breaks out there's a big hassle.
Battlements are on the top of big high walls,
Stairs, doors, rooms, floors and halls.
A very big building,
With lots of shielding.

Robert Jones (7)
Danegrove Primary School, East Barnet

Monster Shredder

Once there was a monster in a deep, dark cave,
If anyone goes in there they will be rather brave.
When he gets in a fight
It carries on all night.
Blood he always drinks, he thinks it's nice,
He never tries anything else like rice.
When he's hungry he likes a treat,
Sometimes he eats human feet.
He always kills things that get in his way,
If they do, they will pay.

Ross Payne (7)
Danegrove Primary School, East Barnet

The Wonderful Weather

Mr Winter was jumping without a sound,
Even on a bunk bed that wasn't very sound.

Then comes Winter, we jump up and down,
Then comes Summer, his head stayed down.

Then comes Autumn with all the leaves,
The leaves were coming down fast and hit his knees.

Then Mr Winter said, 'It's just my sleeves.'
And then he saw the wonderful leaves on his knees.

T J Bruce-Coker (8)
Danegrove Primary School, East Barnet

Lady Summer

Lady Summer comes out of her bed,
Shining on the people putting on suncream.
People sunbathing under the bright sun,
I open my curtains and the sun shines in my house.

Erin Stack (7)
Danegrove Primary School, East Barnet

The Journey Of A River

From the rain up in the sky,
To the mountains there up high,
The shimmering water trickles down so fast,
Then the water splashes into the waterfall, at last.
Slithering, stunning, swishing, thrashing,
The waterfall goes down to the rapids, crashing,
Rapids are crazy, quick and clashing,
As it goes into the sea splashing.
Now the sea is slow and calm,
I pick water droplets up into my palm.

Abita Nanthakumar (11)
Danegrove Primary School, East Barnet

In A Dragon's Cave

Some shiny bones,
A golden coin,
A silver sword,
A brown skeleton,
Some green wood,
A burnt painting,
A ripped up picture,
The front of a book called 'Dragons are Dangerous',
A dragon's roar.

Russell Price (7)
Danegrove Primary School, East Barnet

Lady Summer

Lady Summer is a ball of fire,
The sun makes you sweaty.
People swimming, enjoying the heat.
It is summer,
It burns you,
It is great.

Ronak Ross (7)
Danegrove Primary School, East Barnet

Creation

F reaky creatures
L oves humans for its tea
A different look
N ot normal, very strange!
I n a different kind of world
M ad meaningless animals
A n amazing creation
L oves going to Bogeyland
S melly, old, fat animals.

Afagh Mulazadeh (8)
Danegrove Primary School, East Barnet

Tiger - Haiku

They are very brave.
They're very quick like a plane.
They are in danger.

Jake Langley Burns (7)
Danegrove Primary School, East Barnet

Puppies

They are cheeky,
They are cute,
They are fun to play with
And they'll lay in the sun.

Lucy Carter (7)
Danegrove Primary School, East Barnet

Monsters - Haiku

Monsters eat people
Monsters are always hungry
But they don't like Max.

Max Berlevy (7)
Danegrove Primary School, East Barnet

The Rose

A beautiful rose,
It smells like the gentle breeze,
Soft like a baby.
Red like angry blood,
Sparkly rain on the petals,
All the petals sway.

Micaela Opoku-Mensah (10)
Danegrove Primary School, East Barnet

Valentine's Day

Please give me your heart,
Heart is red for valentines,
Please be my baby,
Don't break my heart,
I love you,
I will be your valentine.

Pauline Ellinas (10)
Danegrove Primary School, East Barnet

My Rabbit - Haiku

My rabbit is fun,
I think he is really fun,
His name is Scooby.

Georgia Chandler (8)
Danegrove Primary School, East Barnet

The Thrashing, Crashing River - Haiku

The thrashing river
Crashes against rocks all day,
Then gently calms down.

Dijon Richmond-Gaisie (11)
Danegrove Primary School, East Barnet

The Sand-Puppy

The beautiful beach lies there, as still as possible,
The sleeping sand-puppy gently awakes.
The sand-puppy's fur so golden and so soft,
As the tourists arrive, the sand-puppy jumps and plays.

The children buy lots of ice creams,
Then drop them onto the floor.
The sand-puppy comes and eats them up
While playing on the shore.

As all the people leave the beach
The sand-puppy feels alone.
He wants to cry, he wants to cry,
So bursts out and soaks himself.

The beach is wet, the beach is cross,
The sand-puppy rules it whole.
He's furious, mad and angry,
But as the time goes by
He falls asleep again.

Sophie Moreton (11)
Danegrove Primary School, East Barnet

The Cliff Dog

On the lonely cliffs, in the gloomy night,
There was a dog that barks at any passers-by,
He growls and groans,
At the nightly wind
And he barks all night.

In the wind he sleeps; he hears a noise.
He looks off the cliffs and he looks at the sea,
He watches the waves hit the cliffs,
As he sleeps and snores, he licks his paws.

Donovan Murfet (11)
Danegrove Primary School, East Barnet

The Emotions Of A River

The angry river is raging,
Burning like a red-hot fire!
Streaming towards the ocean,
Its journey has just begun.

The calm river is quiet,
Flowing so gracefully.
On its adventure towards the ocean,
Silent on its journey.

The happy river is jolly,
Bouncing around to the sea!
Clear and glistening it sparkles,
Amazing, magnificent, breathtaking.

The sad river is moaning,
Slithering away to the sea.
Crashing and bashing the rocks,
Lashing out on anything!

All the rivers are alike,
On their way to the sea!

Jake Nixon (11)
Danegrove Primary School, East Barnet

The River

The flow of the river
It flows down the lane.
Eventually it stops to get its breath back
And travels all over again.
It starts to speed up,
Until the precise moment,
To get to the sea
To find its family
And get something to eat.
When nightfall comes
It rests and sleeps.

Mark Taylor (10)
Danegrove Primary School, East Barnet

A River Poem

The simple brook starts gracefully,
It grows up to be a stream.
Then it gets stronger,
Growing into a river.
Now it's getting as strong as a buffalo,
It goes in the sea, now it's free!
And when you're not happy, it's not happy,
Now it can surely swish up and down.
It's as free as a bird,
With nobody stopping its path.

Nick Adamou (11)
Danegrove Primary School, East Barnet

The River

The calm and peaceful river
Gently vibrating along your skin.
Splashing and crashing against the rocks,
Slowly breaking them into pebbles
And then to sand.
At night it rises as a storm,
Battering boats, sinking them.
No one dares to go in, only fish,
Even then they get washed to the waterfall
And die.

Oren David (10)
Danegrove Primary School, East Barnet

Untitled

The calm gentle river flowing slowly through the light.
When it is vicious you can hear the stones
And bones crashing together.
Orange scaly fishes swimming calmly by the riverbanks,
Splash, the cheerful river jumps quickly as it overlaps the big rocks.

Andrea Panayi (11)
Danegrove Primary School, East Barnet

The Volcano

Throwing the angry lava in the air,
The volcano wolf growls,
Howling, howling looking for a target,
The wolf snarls, looking for its prey,
Scanning the horizon in vain,
He spots his prey - a lonely town
And with a final howl he charges down, down,
Down the mountain, in a puddle of lava,
Destroying the rocks as he goes past,
While the mountain behind him rumbles and growls,
Down to the town, running and running,
Howling and howling, then something amazing happens,
The wind picked up, blocking his way
And there he stops with a howl saying, 'No way!'
He turns away, tail to the ground, feeling upset and down,
But there he turns, and walks away
And so he waits for another day!

Claudia Sarjant (11)
Danegrove Primary School, East Barnet

The River

The river twists and turns like a child who can't get to sleep,
As it lets its water out it overlaps with anger.
Children try and play in the river
But because it's angry it will not let them!
The children shriek with fear!

When the river has calmed down
The children can come out and play.
The river glistens with joy as it has company,
It is very pleasurable to play with.

Because the river is calm it lets the birds drink from its water.
Raindrops start to fall so the children go inside,
The river is left alone.

Claudia Dixon (10)
Danegrove Primary School, East Barnet

The Wind

The wind is like a horse,
Galloping and kicking ferociously,
Knocking over trees and rooftops,
He powerfully surges unseen.

His trots beckon through mountains,
His neighs echo down valleys
And he softly clatters down his fields.

He calmly lays down and causes no harm in early spring,
His calm wind rustles through the trees
And he gently settles down onto the grass.

Peter Michael (11)
Danegrove Primary School, East Barnet

The River

The clear glistening river flows through the woods,
Gracefully twisting and turning.
Nature is by its side watching,
As its current swirls the water along,
Leaves float on top of it,
Whereas pebbles sink to the bottom,
The river slithers under the bridge,
There are ripples in the water where the rain has fallen,
But the river continues till it reaches the sea!

Leah Kline (10)
Danegrove Primary School, East Barnet

My Best Friends And Family

My best friend loves me.
My mum and dad love me a lot.
I love my friends so much.
I love everyone so much.
I like my friends a lot.

Jamie Leanne Ibbott (7)
Danegrove Primary School, East Barnet

The River

The thunderous night river
And tuna, tuna, tuna.
The enormous river cat laughs,
Licking her dangerous paws.

She runs through the furious waves,
Like a stroppy cat slouching on a gloomy day,
She miaows and jumps, frustrated,
The rough river blows!

But when it's warm,
She's shy and velvety smooth,
The cat just lays asleep until the wind awakes her,
The delicate river sleeps!

Holly Tyler (11)
Danegrove Primary School, East Barnet

The River

The furious river crashing into the rocks,
Sometimes he's gentle and sometimes he's angry.
Watch the river float peacefully,
Feel the magnificent nature.

If you're sad the cheerful river will cheer you up,
Look at it bashing and turning into the rocks.
When you look into it, its water is pure,
Hear the waves splash and bash into the rocks.

Marwan Warda (11)
Danegrove Primary School, East Barnet

River

The calm, gentle river is so peaceful,
Crashing against the angry rocks.
The stream is overlapping the strong rocks,
The gentle stream tickling your feet.

Bradley Sayers (10)
Danegrove Primary School, East Barnet

The Wind

The crushing power of hail and howls,
Wind striking fiercely at every tree!
The destructive wind cheetah groans,
Torturing viciously the enormous hounds.
But when the deadly lions roar,
And when the explosive thunder vibrates,
He yawns sleepily and drops to the ground,
And snores rapidly at the destroying wind.
But when the sun comes up again,
It gleams and glows throughout the day,
Awakening the calm, gentle wind,
As it speedily blows all day, all night,
Without a second the settling wind shines
Brightly and smiles, smiles, smiles . . .

James Nesbitt (10)
Danegrove Primary School, East Barnet

The Waves

The crashing, shocking waves
And the vicious strong wave panther
Is ready to pounce on the beach,
The wave panther is as argumentative as can be.

Strong wave panther strikes onto the sea
Like an arrow hitting its target.
The panther soaks the heavy storm with water
As the wave panther changes.

The calm wave cat flows in the night sky,
Still yet soft like a warm blanket.
The wave cat is as happy as can be
And the beautiful calm cat it shall stay.

Amy Pettitt (10)
Danegrove Primary School, East Barnet

Hurt

Hurt can be the end or a new beginning,
It can be a car crash or a baby being born.
Hurt is an animal like a lion killing its prey.
Red is the colour of blood,
It is blood pouring down the motorist's face
As his heart stops and his life flashes before his eyes.
Hurt is when your friends leave you out,
It's when you fall over and graze your knee.
Hurt can be the end or a new beginning.
What do you think hurt can be?

Rebecca Perris (11)
Danegrove Primary School, East Barnet

New Boy

Look at that new kid, all alone,
Face like roses, hair like stone.
Laces like spaghetti, as yellow as can be,
Why do we have new boys? It's such a pity.
Look at that kid, all alone,
Sitting in the corner, eating lunch.
Why don't we invite him over?
'Hey kid come and play.'
'OK.'

Ben Hopkins (9)
Dewhurst St Mary Primary School, Cheshunt

Loneliness Is A Terrible Thing

Loneliness is like a thing that puts stones in your throat,
It punches your heart,
It shreds your happiness,
So you'd better make friends quick
Or loneliness will strike you.
Loneliness is a terrible thing.

Samuel Harris (8)
Dewhurst St Mary Primary School, Cheshunt

My Little Kitten

My little kitten is so cool,
My little kitten is called Mansell.
My little kitten has a pretty face,
My little kitten is full of grace!

My little kitten is so sweet,
My little kitten has four white feet.
My little kitten can be annoying,
My little kitten is never boring!

My little kitten has a wet nose,
My little kitten bites my toes.
My little kitten is soft to touch,
My little kitten I love him so much!

What would I do without him?

Grace Wheeler (11)
Dewhurst St Mary Primary School, Cheshunt

Monkeys

Monkeys are big,
Monkeys are small,
Monkeys are cheeky
And that's not all!

Monkeys are brown,
Monkeys are black,
Give them a banana,
They won't give it back!

Monkeys are playful,
Monkeys are fun,
Monkeys like to jump about
And run, run, run!

Matt Simmons (11)
Dewhurst St Mary Primary School, Cheshunt

Football Fever

The World Cup final's here,
The crowd let out a cheer.
The anthems play,
On this final day,
Supporters filled with fear.

The whistle blows,
The football goes
Up into the air.
Our fingers are crossed,
They think we've lost,
But we're hoping it's our year!

The final minutes are near,
My dad really needs a beer.
It's still nil-nil,
But score we will!
Before the end is here.

Harry Smith (10)
Dewhurst St Mary Primary School, Cheshunt

Unknown

Annoying noise goes creak, creak, creak,
While the mortals try to sleep.
What could it be?
What could it be?

This place is like Hell,
But with a terrible smell.
What could it be?
What could it be?

No drink, no food,
Puts you in a frustrating mood.
What could it be?
What could it be?
For the sake of you and me.

Katharine Keen (10)
Dewhurst St Mary Primary School, Cheshunt

Class Project

I was assigned this class project
Three weeks ago.
I haven't time to do it
Not by tomorrow,
I really don't know
What excuse to use this time!

I'd ask my older brother,
What it's all about.
But he's already left for school,
And cannot help me out!

When I got there, I told my teacher this,
'My baby brother was sick on it.'
And the worst part of it is,
It took me so long to make this up.
I realised with dread
It would have just been easier,
To do the work instead!

Christine Parkins (10)
Dewhurst St Mary Primary School, Cheshunt

Magpies

Magpies flying high,
Magpies high in the sky.
Magpies catching lunch,
Magpies having a munch.
Magpies talking loud,
In a magpie crowd.
Magpies have crisps,
Magpies taking a risk.

That's a magpie's day . . .

Max Newell (11)
Dewhurst St Mary Primary School, Cheshunt

Christmas

C hristmas is a very special time of year,
H olly berries come out at Christmas.
R oses chocolates is what my family likes to eat at Christmas.
I ce is what we slide on at Christmas
S melling the smell of pine cone trees at Christmas.
T rees and chocolates is what you always see around
Christmas time.
M y mum and dad got drunk at Christmas, it was hilarious!
A great present of mine was the Christmas dinner.
S ecretly, I wish we could have Christmas every day.

Lia Mardling (10)
Dewhurst St Mary Primary School, Cheshunt

Seasons Outside

O ut in the garden, in spring we play,
U nder the trees, night and day.
T he beautiful summer flowers in June,
S unbathing on the beach, on the sand dunes.
I n autumn the leaves drop
D own on the ground, left to rot.
E ventually it's winter, that's cold all day.

Jessica Stevenson (10)
Dewhurst St Mary Primary School, Cheshunt

The Ski Trip

S kiing down a slope, I go,
K eeping my balance, on the snow,
I 'm going faster and faster, everywhere I go.
I 'm on a slope, swerving in every direction.
N ow I'm at the bottom of it,
G oing home now.

Charlie Prosser (10)
Dewhurst St Mary Primary School, Cheshunt

The Moon

The moon is like a reflective mirror,
Shining in my eyes.
The moon is peeping through the clouds,
It means evenings are getting nearer.
The moon comes in different sizes.

It's like a big, firm ball
Turning around and around,
We hope it will never fall.
It lives with its brothers and sisters
Called the stars.

Craters crash,
Its home chatters like feet,
As the craters land, they make a huge bash.
The moon can't take the sun's heat.

It's like a round Milky Bar, ready to eat.
It looks like a white tyre.
It's like a white leather seat.
It's like white fire.

It's like refreshing milk.
It glides through the night.
It's like soft silk.
When it's morning it says, 'Bye-bye.'

Jaimal Baxter (8)
Dewhurst St Mary Primary School, Cheshunt

The Predator's Visit

The predator is a hunter,
He only appears at midnight,
He's ready to kill when the night is jet-black,
His dark eye is glimpsed in a lightning flash,
I shut my eyes tight.
He pounds on the ground,
I hear his footsteps crumble the earth,
I weep in shining moonlight.

Joshua Cliss (8)
Dewhurst St Mary Primary School, Cheshunt

Loneliness

When I moved in,
I looked out of the window.
I looked and stared
And saw people everywhere.

But when I went outside,
I saw nobody anywhere.
I looked and looked
And no one was there.

I looked and stared
And no one was there.

I went up and down the street,
I saw no one.
I went to the park
And no one was there.

I looked and stared
And no one was there.

Charlie Murphy (8)
Dewhurst St Mary Primary School, Cheshunt

I Was New

It was horrible, embarrassing,
Like I was a picture,
No friends,
Felt like a statue,
Face like fire.
Down in the dumps,
Down in the playground,
Sad in the classroom,
Scared in school,
Grumpy at home.

Georgia Harrison (8)
Dewhurst St Mary Primary School, Cheshunt

Fashion

Fashion is cool.
Fashion is free.
Fashion is you.
Fashion is me.

All the different makes to choose from
And only the best.
Skirts, trousers, shorts and jeans,
Can't forget the dress.

Fashion for all kinds,
Hot and cold weather,
Some made of silk, some cotton,
Some wool, some made of leather.

Some for partying,
Some for playing football,
Some for the pool,
Or some for just looking cool.

Now we end this wonderful story,
Hope you listen with hope and glory.
You keep up with the trend,
You will find the new you at the end.

Charlotte Franklin (10)
Dewhurst St Mary Primary School, Cheshunt

New Girl

Look at the new girl,
Face like chalk.

Sitting on the bench there,
Just about to talk.

Hair all nice,
Like sugar and spice.

Look at the new girl,
All sad and lonely.

Kitty Newell (9)
Dewhurst St Mary Primary School, Cheshunt

My Family

I have a dad, he is very mad,
He has a bald head like a boiled egg.
I have a dad, he plays rugby
And he is very chubby.

I have a mum, she likes the sun,
She has brown hair like chocolate.
I have a mum, she's the best
But she doesn't like mess.

I have a sister, her name is Rosie
And she is very nosy.
She has blonde hair like the sun.
I have a sister, she's the best
And she also doesn't like mess.

I am the best out of my family.

Alice Hornett (10)
Dewhurst St Mary Primary School, Cheshunt

New School

When I was at my old school,
I kept my head down.
Then I came to this school,
I was filled with joy, all around.
Then I found some friends,
Who liked me for who I am.

When I was a new boy, it was very hard.
When I was new, I was very scared.
But when I found some friends,
I was the happiest boy, all through the land.
When I was a new boy, it was very hard,
When I was new, I was very scared.

Ben Mitchell (8)
Dewhurst St Mary Primary School, Cheshunt

In My Bedroom

I am so scared,
I think it is so scary in here.
I think there is someone in this room,
Outside the owl is hooting
And it is scaring me.
The door is creaking and I don't like it,
I want to go out of this room,
But from the stairs I hear
Tramp, tramp, tramp.

Travis Parker (8)
Dewhurst St Mary Primary School, Cheshunt

The Spirit's Visit

The spirit is a deadly thing.
I'll tell you what it's like.
A murderer from Hell,
Taught how to kill,
Forced to be a malicious monster.
So I would run if I were you,
If it's in your spooky room
And I'd scream if it's you!

Holly Turner (9)
Dewhurst St Mary Primary School, Cheshunt

Lonely

I was lonely
When I was at a club
And I didn't have anybody to play with
And wanted to go home
In my bed.

I was very lonely at the club.

George White (8)
Dewhurst St Mary Primary School, Cheshunt

Loneliness

There was a new boy sitting on the car floor,
He got out of the door,
His face was like stone.

He watched us,
He did nothing,
He'd only just come,
He could still feel Mum's kisses on his face.

New football kit and new boots,
He nearly made a friend,
But he was sent off,
He wanted to go home.

Joe Saul-Baylis (8)
Dewhurst St Mary Primary School, Cheshunt

A New School

When I was at a new school
I was very lonely.
But I made lots of friends
And I played with them every day
And they let me play with them.
Now I have got lots of friends.

Stacey Maunders (9)
Dewhurst St Mary Primary School, Cheshunt

The Moon

The moon rises after the sun goes down,
The holes in it are like ditches in the ground
And the pretty stars make pictures in the sky.
The craters crash with the moon and stars.
The moon is like teeth in the shining light
And fresh milk ready to drink.

Rebecca Evans (9)
Dewhurst St Mary Primary School, Cheshunt

Getting Scared?

At the top of the stairs,
The evil thing is waiting for me.

There's a monster in my wardrobe,
There's a monster in my bed,
It's breathing in my head.

I recklessly step towards the top stair
Where he swings at my hair.

There's a monster in my wardrobe,
There's a monster in my bed,
It's breathing in my head.

I swing round, I hurtle away,
I thought he was going to swipe my head.

There's a monster in my wardrobe,
There's a monster in my bed,
It's breathing in my head.

Whispery and glowing, with eyes aflame,
My heart a-beating like a drum, I scream.

There's a monster in my wardrobe,
There's a monster in my bed,
It's breathing in my head.

It chases me back down the stairs,
I feel I dread this night.

There's a monster in my wardrobe,
There's a monster in my bed,
It's breathing in my head.

It laughs at its evil schemes,
It locks fears in my head.

There's a monster in my wardrobe,
There's a monster in my bed,
It's breathing in my head.

Tommy Hunn (8)
Dewhurst St Mary Primary School, Cheshunt

Flowers

Flowers are green,
Flowers are red,
Flowers are everywhere.

Flowers are smelly,
Flowers are pretty,
Flowers are blue and green.

Flowers are big,
Flowers are small,
Flowers are all sizes.

Flowers are green,
Flowers are red,
Flowers are all colours.

Flowers are the best.

Emelia Montanari (9)
Dewhurst St Mary Primary School, Cheshunt

The Moon

The moon is like chocolate, ready to eat.
Shining in the sky.
It's like cheese, full of wheat,
When it goes down it says, 'Goodbye!'

The good moon,
The bad moon,
The always white moon.

The moon is white, like milk,
It lights up the sky.
It's like a big ball of silk,
Even though it's up so high.

Lauren Burton (9)
Dewhurst St Mary Primary School, Cheshunt

Loneliness

When I was lonely, I was scared
So I went to my dad and he said,
'Go outside, ride your bike.
And make some friends.'

So I went outside, and played outside
And I was scared.
A boy came and said,
'Come and play with me,'
But I was too scared to say yes.

Then I remembered
What my dad said.
I said, 'Yes!'
And we became
Best friends.

Fuat Ahmet (9)
Dewhurst St Mary Primary School, Cheshunt

The Year

January is jumping around,
February is like frosty paths,
March is windy days,
April is daffodils and tulips,
May is for May Day,
June is like the sun,
July is break up for summer holidays,
August is awesome fun at the seaside,
September is autumn leaves,
October is Hallowe'en,
November is fireworks,
December is Christmas, *hooray!*

Leah Fisher (9)
Dewhurst St Mary Primary School, Cheshunt

Ten Foul Fish

(Inspired by 'Ten Little Schoolboys' by A A Milne)

Ten foul fish swimming in the sea,
One saw a shark and decided to flee.

Nine foul fish looking for some food.
One saw McDonald's and a burger he chewed.

Eight foul fish out for trick or treat,
One saw a sweet and off he went to eat.

Seven foul fish looking for a pet,
One got caught in a fishing net.

Six foul fish running in a race,
One tripped over, fell flat on his face.

Five foul fish went to have a look,
Oh no! one got stuck on a fishing hook.

Four foul fish playing a video game,
One took a walk and saw a pretty dame.

Three foul fish playing with a toy.
Then the girlie fish saw a handsome boy.

Two foul fish playing a game of snap,
Then one got caught in a lobster trap.

One foul fish talking on the phone,
Took a look behind and saw he was alone.

Joseph Pinkney (10)
Dewhurst St Mary Primary School, Cheshunt

The Moon

The moon is good enough to eat,
It's as white as white can be,
It's when the day and night meets,
It's like a bubble stuck together.
The moon looks like a massive football,
It's like white chocolate, ready to eat.

Luke Aspland (9)
Dewhurst St Mary Primary School, Cheshunt

Big Brothers, Little Sisters

Big brothers, little sisters,
I have two of each.
I'm stuck in the middle,
Like shells on a beach.

Big brothers are annoying
They spoil all my games,
They pick on me,
And they call me names.

Little sisters aren't much better,
They're not as sweet as they look!
They ruin all my make-up,
And mess up all my books.

Big brothers can be good,
They help when I am in a muddle.
And if I ever get upset,
They give me a big cuddle.

Little sisters can be sweet,
They like to hold my hand.
They sing funny little songs,
When they are playing in the sand.

Big brothers, little sisters,
Really aren't too bad,
But I still can't help it
They really make me *mad!*

Shelby Fraser (10)
Dewhurst St Mary Primary School, Cheshunt

The Moon

The moon is a shiny ball,
Floating in the sky.
Shining in my eyes,
It glides through the sky.

Reuben Gatens (8)
Dewhurst St Mary Primary School, Cheshunt

The Dentist

Today was the day that I really fear,
I'm off to the dentist. Oh dear . . .
As I got in the car, I pictured it in my head,
This is the place that I really dread.

We drove off right down the lane,
I could already feel the pain.
Oh no, we're nearly there,
I'll soon be getting in that horrid chair.

As we walk through the door,
All I did was look at the floor.
As I sat there, I heard the drill,
It was me next, with my tooth to fill.

I hopped in the chair and saw a light,
I trembled with fear, oh what a sight.
I opened my mouth, the dentist looked in,
He looked at me with a great grin.

'Your teeth are just fine.
Please come back another time.
There is nothing to fear,
Come back next year.'

Emily Phillips (10)
Dewhurst St Mary Primary School, Cheshunt

Loneliness

I started school one day
I didn't want to go
Because I didn't know anybody there.

But my mum forced me to,
So I went to school.

I saw people playing,
So I went to play with them,
Then we were friends. Forever.

Matthew Ball (8)
Dewhurst St Mary Primary School, Cheshunt

My Teddy Bear Story

The bear on my bed,
Has a furry head.
We sleep together by the door,
But in the morning he's all alone, on the floor.
I say his colour is brown,
But my mum says he's gold, like a crown
He has a bent ear
And no fur on his rear.
He's got a big tummy
I think he must have eaten lots of honey.
His name is Ed,
Cos it seemed a good name for a ted.
When I saw him in the shop,
I wanted him so much, I threw a strop!
He has been with me
Since I wore a nappy.

Abbie Ward (9)
Dewhurst St Mary Primary School, Cheshunt

A Day All Alone

New girl on her own,
Rosy cheeks, as
Still as stone.
Crystal blue eyes, looking
At the clear blue sky.

Other children singing songs,
All look at the new girl,
Sitting on her own.
She wants to stay at home
But she wishes she could be out, singing songs,
And be with all the other kids
Having fun.

Vanessa Coomes (8)
Dewhurst St Mary Primary School, Cheshunt

Loneliness

Look at him
Face like stone
No one to play with
Hair's all straight.
Poor, poor him
Lost his smile.

When I got home
My mum was smiling.
I told her I was worried
When I was at school.
I never got a friend
I was too shy
I was too scared to ask.

'I bet tomorrow you will get a friend.'

Taylor Jermy (9)
Dewhurst St Mary Primary School, Cheshunt

Loneliness

Lonely boy sitting there
Like rock-hard stone
Because he keeps hiding.

He will not play
Because his mum kisses him all over
And he's embarrassed.

I'm embarrassed because
Of my mum's great big kisses.
That's why the children won't play with me,
I think.

Glenn Miller (8)
Dewhurst St Mary Primary School, Cheshunt

The Savage Scorpion

This creature devours,
with phenomenal powers.
Using monstrous claws
and a toxic tail that no prey endures.

A swift black knight,
coated in armour,
wielding a poisonous dagger,
stabbing its victim with intense valour.

Bone crushing pincers
that you cannot defy,
dominating its foe
in the blink of an eye.

The Arabian fat-tailed scorpion.

Jamie Bain (10)
Dewhurst St Mary Primary School, Cheshunt

Football Crazy

Football crazy, football mad,
Muddy boots and dirty knees.
Screaming and shouting from everyone.
Left foot, right foot,
Down the line.
Ouch! that hurt.
I've slipped in the dirt.
Up on my feet, looking cool.
Take a shot, straight at the goal.
In it goes, oh what a shot!

Liam O'Leary (10)
Dewhurst St Mary Primary School, Cheshunt

My Brother

Some brothers are cute,
Some brothers are funny,
Some brothers can play the flute,
And make your day sunny.

But my brother's nothing like that,
He's actually better, in fact,
Although he is my brother
I love him
Just like that!

Aimee Bracebridge (11)
Dewhurst St Mary Primary School, Cheshunt

Loneliness

If you're lonely, you feel heartbroken,
If you're lonely, you feel lovebroken,
If you're scared, you don't feel cared for.
If you're lonely you feel sad,
You surely won't feel glad!
If you're lonely you feel bad,
You surely won't feel glad!
So please have a go,
You really don't know!

Chas Flynn (9)
Dewhurst St Mary Primary School, Cheshunt

About Kate

K ate is great fun,
A nd is very funny. She
T alks to lots of people,
E ven when she is on holiday!

Kate Charlton (10)
Dewhurst St Mary Primary School, Cheshunt

Ten Little Fishes

(Inspired by 'Ten Little Schoolboys' by A A Milne)

Ten little fishes swimming in a line,
One jumped out and then there were nine.

Nine little fishes shouting about their date.
One swam in a circle and then there were eight.

Eight little fishes all sleeping in Heaven,
One floated up to God and then there were seven.

Seven little fishes one choked on a stick,
He had a heart attack and then there were six.

Six little fishes eating their Weetabix
One went to the toilet and then there were five.

Five little fishes looking for more.
One got lost and then there were four.

Four little fishes looking at me
He was flying in the sky, then there were three.

Three little fishes one shouted, 'Boo!'
One ran away and then there were two.

Two little fishes, I want none
So he had none and then there was one.

One little fish, he said, 'I'm just the one.'
He died so then there were none.

Freddie Stevenson (8)
Dewhurst St Mary Primary School, Cheshunt

New School

I was frightened
When I went to this school
Because no one wanted
To play with me.

I sat on the friendship bench
And I cried.

Ria Graham (9)
Dewhurst St Mary Primary School, Cheshunt

Ten Little Kittens

(Inspired by 'Ten Little Schoolboys' by A A Milne)

Ten little kittens,
Squeaking in a line,
One fell over and then there were nine.

Nine little kittens,
Saw a scary gate,
One ran away, then there were eight.

Eight little kittens,
All in Heaven,
One fell out, then there were seven.

Seven little kittens,
Picking up sticks,
One went home, then there were six.

Six little kittens,
All having a dive,
One went home, then there were five.

Five little kittens,
Banging on the door,
One went to sleep, then there were four.

Four little kittens,
Had a little bee,
One got stung and then there were three.

Three little kittens,
All in a big shoe,
They went to sleep and then there were two.

Two little kittens,
Having a big bun,
One had too much, then there was one.

One little kitten,
Is the only hero,
She saved the world and then there were zero.

Cody T Chamberlain (8)
Dewhurst St Mary Primary School, Cheshunt

Ten Little Rats

(Inspired by 'Ten Little Schoolboys' by A A Milne)

Ten little rats looking so fine,
One got eaten by a cat,
Then there were nine.

Nine little rats saw their gate,
One fell over,
Then there were eight.

Eight little rats sitting in Heaven,
One died quickly,
Then there were seven.

Seven little rats watching some tricks,
One got hurt,
Then there were six.

Six little rats all alive,
One had a heart attack,
Then there were five.

Five little rats wanting much more,
One went fishing,
Then there were four.

Four little rats forgot their key,
One went home,
Then there were three.

Three little rats wearing their shoes,
One fell off,
Then there were two.

Two little rats having fun.
One went off,
Then there was one.

One little rat filled his tum,
Then he died,
And there were none!

Abi Fisher (8)
Dewhurst St Mary Primary School, Cheshunt

Ten Little Cats

(Inspired by 'Ten Little Schoolboys' by A A Milne)

Ten little cats, feeling all fine,
And then came a storm
Then there were nine.

Nine little cats, they were all late,
One got left out
And then there were eight.

Eight little cats, one went to Heaven,
He didn't come down
And then there were seven.

Seven little cats, all doing tricks,
One fell over
And then there were six.

Six little cats, went for a dive,
One was too scared
And then there were five.

Five little cats, opened the door,
One was shot
And then there were four.

Four little cats, one climbed up a tree,
He got stuck
And then there were three.

Three little cats, one had the flu,
He had to stay in bed
And then there were two.

Two little cats, they had some fun,
One bumped his head
And then there was one.

One little cat, was a hero,
But then he fell
And then there were zero.

Nicole Mcliveney (8)
Dewhurst St Mary Primary School, Cheshunt

Snow Is Here

Snow is here,
Snow is there,
Snow is undoubtedly everywhere.

The snow that falls is crispy white
And falls all through the day and night.

Snow is here,
Snow is there,
Snow is undoubtedly everywhere.

Snow is a blanket that never keeps you warm,
It travels by wind, rain or storm.

Snow is here,
Snow is there,
Snow is undoubtedly everywhere.

Snow, snow, snow, the wind does blow,
As snowballs fly and sledges go.

Snow is here,
Snow is there,
Snow is undoubtedly everywhere.

The sun is out, the children shout,
The snow is melting, around about.

Snow is here,
Snow is there,
Snow is undoubtedly everywhere.

Which leaves me to say . . .
We'll wait till it snows, another day!

Jack Morter (11)
Dewhurst St Mary Primary School, Cheshunt

Friends Are Great!

F riends are loyal,
R eally great to be with,
I ntelligent,
E ncouraging,
N ever unfaithful,
D efinitely the greatest to be with,
S urely the best to be around.

A round when you're down,
R eally fun,
E xciting.

G roovy,
R eally friendly,
E legant,
A wesome,
T actful.

Alisha Buckle & Jessica Morrell (11)
Dewhurst St Mary Primary School, Cheshunt

Best Friends

B est friends till the end
E mily is good as gold.
S unny days are the best day for us.
T hen the snow falls, another great day.

F or us we play till sun falls,
R un around enjoying the day.
I n each other's houses, all day long.
E lena is good as gold.
N ow what will we do next?
D ays have past, what shall we do?
S o now we're stuck, bored again!

Elena Pelech (10)
Dewhurst St Mary Primary School, Cheshunt

Christmas Time Is Now Here

Christmas time is now here,
Wrap up warm and begin to cheer.
Have a laugh and have some fun,
Christmas has only just begun.
Your presents are there, under the tree.
Look at them there, they are mostly for me.
Carol-singers are here and there,
Trying to get a Christmas share.
Come the evening, snow may fall,
And a good time will be had by all.
Making snowmen and snowballs,
Wet wellingtons in the halls.
Roast turkey and stuffing on my plate,
I sniff the air, the smell is great.
I toast you with ginger beer,
Merry Christmas and a happy New Year.

Rachel Howes (10)
Dewhurst St Mary Primary School, Cheshunt

My Poem

Today I am a basketball player,
Like a miniature Michael Jordan,
An impressive and popular player.

Today I am a tennis player,
Like a miniature Tim Henman,
Sensational and gifted.

Today I am a footballer,
Like a miniature Thierry Henry,
Skilful and intelligent performer.

Sam Chaney (10)
Dewhurst St Mary Primary School, Cheshunt

The Moon

Evening's coming
The sun is dying
It's bright tonight.

Our moon is our moon, gliding in the sky.
Our moon looks good enough to eat.
Floating in the big blue sky.

Our moon is our moon, gliding in the sky.
Craters crash, leaving gaping holes,
Covering the surface.

Our moon is our moon, gliding in the sky,
Our moon is as white as toothpaste.
Our moon is our moon, gliding in the sky.
It makes me think of blueberry pie,
Floating in the big blue sky.

Our moon is our moon
For us.

Warwick Byrne (9)
Dewhurst St Mary Primary School, Cheshunt

The Girl Thing

A girl needs her looks and a great sense of fashion.
With make-up and jewels and some attitude and passion.

Girls need their make-up, loads of it, heaps,
Girls need their excitement and beauty sleep.

They need their share of shopping with bling and cash of course.
And maybe buy a puppy or maybe a horse.

So if you need advice, just ask me for some more,
And maybe next time I'll take you on a tour.

Chelsea Helmond-Jones (9)
Dewhurst St Mary Primary School, Cheshunt

The Hand's Visit

The hand is a dreadful thing
It creeps in the night.
It is the most deadly thing on the Earth
Tonight its shadow is on the wall.

I see a ghoul in the shadow,
It stirs, it squeals.
I look, I stare,
A door swings open.
I see a face which scares me.
I shut my eyes
And wish it would go away.

My peeping eyes spy on it,
It will not go away
And then I leap out of my bed.
Get a creeepy book and put it on the floor.
All the horrible things are sucked inside the book
And will never get out again.

Paige Burgess (8)
Dewhurst St Mary Primary School, Cheshunt

Speed

Speed you're so fast,
As the day's going past.
Speed is so fast,
But you also come last.
Speed can be slow,
Like when tying a bow.
Speed can be a risk,
Like a round spinning disk.
People often go fast,
But they'll end up in a cast.

Kerris Mezen (9)
Dewhurst St Mary Primary School, Cheshunt

Horse Riding

I like riding
I think it's fun,
Sit and trot! Sit and trot!
And then we have to run.
All different types of ponies,
All different colours.

Instructions by my teacher,
Who helps me to ride.
I like my teacher,
She is very kind.

My horse is called Spot,
She is very fast,
I love going riding, it is fun.

Lauren Taylor (10)
Dewhurst St Mary Primary School, Cheshunt

Pillow Fights

Whack, whack!
Avoiding pillow after pillow
Whack, whack!
Launched my attack on a unsuspecting friend
Whack, whack!
Knocked to the floor again and again but
Keep on coming back, again and again.
Whack, whack!
It's the final blows and I hope I'm the last one standing.
Fomf, fomf!
We're on the floor now and laughing our heads off,
Because this is the perfect way to end our sleepover.
Ha, ha!

Elizabeth Easterbrook (10)
Dewhurst St Mary Primary School, Cheshunt

Black Hole

B lack holes are giants eating planets and light,
L iving in space is like an antigravity machine,
A liens killing all visitors like a soldier in a war,
C omets inhabited by nuclear craters,
K iller aliens destroy planets like murderers destroy people.

H umans fighting over the galaxy like toddlers over a toy,
O ver the years the galaxy overheated like the atom bomb in Japan,
L ess and less of the aliens existed, Earth may survive,
E arth won the galactic war! What may happen next . . . ?

Jamie Thomas (10)
Dewhurst St Mary Primary School, Cheshunt

Untitled

War is a headache which is not going away.
War is a shark circling its prey.
War is a bullet flying through the air.
War is a gun firing at a bear.

Water is blue, teaming with fish.
Water is enormous and salty.
Water is a cold, fresh drink.
Water is ice-cold and bitter.

School is tiring, I lie on my bed when I get home.
School is sometimes fun.
School is friends to play with.
School is a learning place.

Josh Rimmer (10)
Fairhaven CE (VA) Primary School, South Walsham

My View Of Things

Friends are the walking stick of the old man
   are the helpers in class.

Fun is the laughter of the child
   is the scent in the air.

Hell is the gun in life
   is the hate of the Devil.

Heaven is the rose of the bunch
   is the kindness of God.

Terrorists are the evil in the night
   are the demons on Earth.

Mums are the kisses at bedtime
   are the solvers of troubles.

Audie Warren (11)
Fairhaven CE (VA) Primary School, South Walsham

Untitled

Murder is a knife in the back
   is the scent of vengeance

Sport is a hedgerow of games
   is a never-ending game

Nature is a never-ending life cycle
   is a land where animals roam

Death is a sad part of life
   is a part of growing up

Holiday is a suitcase of surprise
   is a great time of joy.

William Ives (10)
Fairhaven CE (VA) Primary School, South Walsham

Caribbean Poems

Pirate is a black soul in my mind,
    is the ghost of midnight.

Market is a burst of colours and surprises,
    is a hurricane of noise.

Sea is a morning blue, glistening in the sun,
    is mixed emotions, peacefully flowing.

Fruit is a juicy smile on my face,
    is the magic world of taste.

Lightning crackling and sparkling,
    skies alight with silver rage.

Jessica Futter (11)
Fairhaven CE (VA) Primary School, South Walsham

Things I Know

Peace is a flower in bloom,
    is the scent of a rose.
A clock is someone waving,
    is a drip of a tap.
A bed is a big marshmallow,
    is a soft fluffy cloud.
A fruit bowl is a colourful rainbow,
    is the smell of summer days.
A snail is a statue,
    is a sleeping cat.
The sky is a big umbrella,
    is a sparkly curtain at night.

Emma Rose (10)
Fairhaven CE (VA) Primary School, South Walsham

My Ideas

Flame is an orange flare
    is the scent of burning

War is the world, fighting
    is the sound of guns

Happiness is people laughing
    is the sound of a happy voice

Homework is children crying
    they don't want to do it

Children playing games in the street
    having fun

Mess is things everywhere
    dirty mess everywhere

Food, it sits in your fridge
    it waits to be eaten.

James Starkings (9)
Fairhaven CE (VA) Primary School, South Walsham

Seaside

The tide is pushing against the pebbles.
Making patterns in the sand.
The wind is so strong it nearly blows you away,
People hanging on to their windbreaks.
A yummy picnic for the family lunch,
With added sand, it makes it crunch.
Children having fun in the sea,
Nearly time to go home for tea.
Packing all the things away,
Can we come back another day?

Claire Edwards (10)
Fairhaven CE (VA) Primary School, South Walsham

The Nice Things In The World

Peace is a flower in bloom
    is the scent of a rose.

Night-time is as dark as coal
    especially when the moon is covered
    by a thick black cloud.

Sheep are soft and cuddly,
    they are as soft as fluffy marshmallows
    with black liquorice feet.

Ravens are flying in the air,
    their wings swiftly flapping.

Skyscrapers stand tall in the sky
    looking out of the window
    and people looking like ants.

Children are playing in the park,
    running around, playing sharks.

Shannon Mills (9)
Fairhaven CE (VA) Primary School, South Walsham

Things I Know

Peace is a flower in bloom
    is the scent of a rose
War is the ache in my mind
    is the bruise on my heart
Food is the filling in my belly
    is the taste in my mouth
Sunshine is the light from God
    is the heat of the world
Wind is the breeze on my skin
    is the pressure in the air.

Katherine Lund (10)
Fairhaven CE (VA) Primary School, South Walsham

The Things I Think About

Peace is a flower in bloom
      is the scent of a rose.

Cat is the cushion that I sleep on
      is my old friend.

Bed is my luxury item
      is my resting place.

House is my home of love
      is my protection and my shield.

Sound is the noise that I dread
      is the evil flower in the bed.

Dirt is the thing that my mum dreads
      is the evil within.

Michael Cole (11)
Fairhaven CE (VA) Primary School, South Walsham

Happiness

War is a blade of a knife
      is the end of a thistle

Exercise is the health of an apple
      is the ripeness of a banana

Friendship is the joy of sharing
      is the sun of a summer's day

Death is the blade of an axe
      is the sting of a wasp

Happiness is the joy of a new pet
      is the colours of the rainbow.

Robert Lee (10)
Fairhaven CE (VA) Primary School, South Walsham

What It Means To Me

The sun
    is the sea, it looks like
    a flashing diamond.

Bombs are
    the pit in my stomach
    the pain in my heart.

Flowers are
    the birds singing
    the glittering sun in the sky.

The people sitting on the streets
    is the cruelty in this world,
    the tears of a man
    the fears of a girl.

Katy Cooper (9)
Fairhaven CE (VA) Primary School, South Walsham

Things I Like

I laugh at bears
when they fall down the stairs

Dogs are funny
when they scratch their tummy

Fat cats
chase rats

Flowers are beautiful
with a lovely scent

Hello Honey,
I want your money.

Natasha Church (10)
Fairhaven CE (VA) Primary School, South Walsham

The Animals' Zoo

Cats
>
> They are fluffy and cute
> they are fun to play with.

Birds
>
> They are cute and fun
> and they love to sing.

Mice
>
> They are fun and playful
> and they run really fast.

Dogs
>
> They are funny and nice
> and love to play football.

Hamsters
>
> They are funny and playful
> they run in their ball.

Steven Freer (11)
Fairhaven CE (VA) Primary School, South Walsham

My Favourite Sports

Tennis is a skilful sport
> is full of concentration

Cricket is a ball game
> is full of energy

Rugby is a rough sport
> is full of contact

Basketball is a reflex game
> is full of accuracy.

James Hodgson (10)
Fairhaven CE (VA) Primary School, South Walsham

My Ideas

War is a gunshot to the head
  is a bullet to the heart

Heaven is like being in a safe house
  is a roller coaster you've just got to ride it

Hell is like a prison, there's no way out
  is a stomach - putrid and vile.

A rainbow is a pathway to happiness
  is an angel of light.

A dog is like a bundle of joy
  will be your friend for life.

Sean Blyth (10)
Fairhaven CE (VA) Primary School, South Walsham

War Is Bad

War is a gravestone in the ground
  is the ghost of a man.

Happiness is a joyful thing
  is a violet's petal.

Sadness is a dinner I don't like
  is a monster in my bed.

Sickness is a war in your stomach
  is a piranha eating you alive.

Love is a flower with a friend
  is a friendship of two.

Jac Hudson (10)
Fairhaven CE (VA) Primary School, South Walsham

My Interest

Football is great to watch,
is entertaining.
Television programmes are full of information,
are fun to watch.
A chair is fun to sit on,
takes all the weight off your legs.
A bed is great to sleep on,
is soft and warm.
Clothes keep me warm when it's cold,
make you look good.

Tom Goodrum (10)
Fairhaven CE (VA) Primary School, South Walsham

My Cheetah Mum

My mum is like a cheetah
pouncing on its prey.
So I'm warning you, you'd best keep away.

So you shouldn't go near her
'cause she will get fiercer.
So I wouldn't turn around because she might eat ya.

Nobody can stop her
if you would like to try,
go on step aside.
But as soon as you go in there,
you won't come back alive.

So I'm warning you
don't go near her side.

Perry McNally (10)
Ferrars Junior School, Luton

Anger!

Anger is as red as hot flames making a house
burn down to the ground.
It sounds like terrorist bombs
in my head.
It reminds me of a lion ripping
into its prey.
It looks like a child running away from the
danger, dripping with blood.
It tastes like the child's blood pouring
down my throat.
It smells like an animal left to die
and rot away.
It feels like a hyena biting its
way through me.

Lee Thorne (10)
Ferrars Junior School, Luton

Laughter

Laughter is sky-blue. It's like birds singing sweetly,
While gliding smoothly in the air.
It looks like a field full of red, elegant roses.
It feels as soft as fluffy, furry cushions.
It reminds me of a big family celebration.
It sounds like a saxophone jazzing its way to freedom.

Iffra Rashid (10)
Ferrars Junior School, Luton

Anger

Anger is as red as blood.
It sounds like a bomb exploding.
It reminds me of a raging fire.
It tastes like a red-hot chilli pepper.
It feels like a fireball going down my throat.

Kyle Dwyer (10)
Ferrars Junior School, Luton

The Weird Dog

The weird dog
Is a funny little joker.
He got up in the morning and started playing poker.
He's like a big, hairy bear,
But he doesn't give a care.

He's like a loud bomb
Talking all the time.
I wish he would be quiet,
So I can get on with this rhyme.

He's like a kangaroo bouncing up and down.
He's so full of life,
It's like standing next to a clown.

I take him out for a walk
And surprise, surprise, he starts to talk.
He's the weirdest dog you could ever have.
His skin is like a horse's, pale, light brown
And still he will be shouting
Even in the town.

Timothy Mutton (11)
Ferrars Junior School, Luton

My Mum Is Like A Lion

My mum is like a lion,
She roars like a hungry one.
When she's angry it's like she pounces on her prey.
When she is shouting you'd best keep away.
I'm warning you keep away.
She might beat you and eat you,
You'd best stay away if you want to live.
She is a lion.

Jade Wakelin (11)
Ferrars Junior School, Luton

Football

Thierry Henry is as fast as a bullet.
Ronaldinho is as skilful as the world's
best race car driver.
Samuel Eto'o scores goals for fun like Tom Cruise
shooting people in his movies.

Roberto Carlos hits the post like a bomb
blowing up in the sea.
Zidane has vision like a lion about to kill his prey.

Dida saves penalties like a mind-reader.
Toura is determined to make sure that no one
gets past him like the world's best runner,
determined to win.

Adriano's accuracy is like the world's best gun shooter.
Deco is a free-kick robot, he never misses.

C Ronaldo makes mind-blowing crosses
Ribinho has stamina like a cheetah.
Essien has the strength of a wild bull.

Jahny'e Knight (11)
Ferrars Junior School, Luton

Fire

Fire is red snakes dancing,
Like red rubies gleaming.
Orange suns glow in the middle of the fire,
As they cling to the red snakes.
The last part of the fire is yellow,
The shiniest of all the colours.
Yellow lemons at the bottom of the orange
                              fascinates me more.
The fire is like a sunset in the sky,
Until I watch it burn to ash.

Zhane Kilby (10)
Ferrars Junior School, Luton

The Journey

I stepped on the platform,
Scared as a rabbit being chased by an eagle.
I thought, *what if I go to a place where no one likes me?*
I climbed onto the train,
So scared I was shaking so hard,
I was nearly unable to grip onto the handrail.

When they asked me to show them my ticket,
I could hardly take my hands out of my pockets.
I sat down in a seat,
The only one left,
It had rips on the side
And was very uncomfortable.

I saw the countryside, nearly there!
I dreaded the moment of getting off,
Finding out who I'd got.
I traipsed off the platform, wobbly on my legs,
But my journey had only just begun,
I had no idea where I was going next!

Sarah Dempsey (9)
Ferrars Junior School, Luton

My Dirt Bike

I ride a dirt bike
That I really like.
It's also very fast,
Like a rocket launcher blast.
I do jumps
And ride on bumps.
It barks like a guard dog.
But when there is no petrol it sounds like a hog.
It's bright green,
Like you have never seen.
There are so many great feels
While I am riding on my bright silver wheels.
After all it is a dirt bike.

Raees Khan (11)
Ferrars Junior School, Luton

Evacuation

The chills down my spine make me nervous,
As I am pushed around the platform,
Like I'm invisible.
As I get on the train my nerves go down,
I have found a place of comfort,
I never want to leave this place,
It is my home now.
When we get to the next platform,
I don't want to get off.

I see a nice family staring at me,
Like they want to take me home.
As I walk to my new family's home I see a river,
It reminds me when I was with my mother,
Playing in the water.
I think about my parents
Every time I close my eyes,
If only I could see them again,
My spirits would be lifted and happiness would be in my heart.

Andrew Brooks (10)
Ferrars Junior School, Luton

My Fierce Crosser

My fierce crosser
Can fly like a rocket
Fast as a cheetah
Or even a bullet.

When I ride my crosser I'm invisible
The wind hammers my face
And my wheels are screeching.

It sounds like a roaring lion
And accelerates as fast as an aeroplane
Rides as smooth as baby skin.

Christopher Gray (11)
Ferrars Junior School, Luton

The City Of Babylon

Arrow flying in the air to hit its target.
Fire everywhere.
Sands of time rushing everywhere to kill.
Sand demons rushing by, hunting their prey
like a lion in the jungle.
Blood splashing on the floor like a bottle
of wine spilt.
There is nothing left of Babylon except
dead bodies lying around.
Houses trashed, Babylon poisoned and ruined.
The war is not over.
Crash!
Arrows set houses on fire.
For this is the end of the mighty city.

Mohammed Nabeel Asghar (10)
Ferrars Junior School, Luton

My Sister

My sister, my sister is a mouse, small and cunning,
She's a snake, sneaking up on you when you least expect it.

My sister, my sister likes changing her clothes four times a day,
When she wears them she's as proud as a peacock,
Her favourite words are, 'Let's go shopping.'
My sister is a thief. Her motto is,
'What's yours is ours, what's mine is mine.'

My sister thinks she's older than me,
My sister is almost as bossy as me,
My sister, my sister is an annoying little rat,
But I love my sister and I never want her to change.

Monica Mangoro (10)
Ferrars Junior School, Luton

Bugatti

The Bugatti is the king of the road car world,
Like a cheetah which is the fastest of the animal world.
Its spine-chilling soundtrack from the exhaust is deafening,
It accelerates at the speed of light.
The ruler of all engines.
The interior is as luxurious as 50 Cent's house,
Smelling the leather is mind-blowing.
The rear tyres are frustratingly wide as a tennis court.
Feel the immense power running down your back.
Turn on the engine and it shocks you half to death.

Rhys Davies (11)
Ferrars Junior School, Luton

My Friend

My friend is a cheeky monkey,
Likes Lamborghini and Escolades,
Is as fast as a tiger,
Acts like a clown, always mucking around.

Has eyes as dark as tree bark.
Always got a cheeky grin on him.
Like a cheetah getting ready to catch the prey.
My friend has a soft heart every now and then.
My friend is Romaro.

Nadia Ahmed (10)
Ferrars Junior School, Luton

Teddy Bear Ballet

Twirling so very gracefully like swans,
Jumping and landing so lightly we can't hear.
Pouncing as high as the moon.
Sounds of squealing when getting things right.

Laura Colclough (11)
Ferrars Junior School, Luton

Cheetah

The king of speed throughout the jungle,
like a firework out of control.
He is always ready to catch his prey
at the speed of sound.
Cross his path and you'll be stunned.
His fur is as smooth as a kitten's back.
As powerful as an untamed fire.
His mighty power sends animals scurrying.
Beware! He's silent but deadly.

Tristan Owen (11)
Ferrars Junior School, Luton

My Cousin's Room

Big, quiet, still and pink,
with pictures of famous celebrities on her door.
Her perfume is like a new flower that has
just blossomed on a tree.
She tweets like a beautiful singing bird
at the break of day.
As we sing and dance happily around her big room.
We laugh like happy butterflies.

Olivia Popoola (10)
Ferrars Junior School, Luton

Luton Town

Luton score, Luton roar,
Luton are like tigers, prowling and growling.
Luton are boaters, flying in the wind,
Luton are like kings and queens
Ruling the pitch like lions, jumping on the ball.
Luton are heroes to me,
But a lot of people don't see.

Victoria Adkins (10)
Ferrars Junior School, Luton

Laughter

Laughter is as bright as the golden sun,
It sounds like bells ringing,
It reminds me of my best friends,
It makes me ecstatic,
It smells like air freshener,
It tastes like ice cream melting in my mouth,
And feels like me laying my head against
My pillow at night when I'm really tired.

Selva Ross (11)
Ferrars Junior School, Luton

Happiness

Happiness is as yellow as the sun,
It sounds like the calm sea coming in and going out,
It feels like ice cream melting in my mouth,
It looks like a puppy running around,
It tastes like chocolate cake,
It smells like a field full of flowers,
It reminds me of the beach and the sea.

Grace Burch (10)
Ferrars Junior School, Luton

Hate

Hate is black like a bottomless well.
It sounds like cymbals bashing at my ears.
It reminds me of a serpent suffocating its prey.
It smells like rotten flesh.
It tastes like sour lemons.
It feels like a lion bit my hand off.

Kier Buot (11)
Ferrars Junior School, Luton

Happiness

Happiness is the colour yellow.
Happiness feels like a soft kitten.
Happiness sounds like children playing.
Happiness reminds me of summer.
Happiness looks like a newborn baby.
Happiness tastes like a chocolate cake.
Happiness smells like the freshly cut grass in the summer.

Lucy Mardell (10)
Ferrars Junior School, Luton

Hate

Hate is red, like blood shot,
when your best friend shoots you
with a bullet going through your heart.
It sounds like a bullet exploding.
It looks like blood squirting out of you.
It smells like blood dropping off a wall.
It tastes like blood in your mouth.

Jeremy Aytoun (12)
Ferrars Junior School, Luton

Love

Love is as pink as a blooming rose.
It sounds like birds singing in the sunny air.
It reminds me of big angel love hearts.
It smells like new growing daisies.
It feels like someone kissing me.
It tastes like melted chocolate.

Rachel Brown (10)
Ferrars Junior School, Luton

Treasure Chest

Treasure chest bring me some gold.
Treasure chest bring me some silver.
Make the silver and gold real.
Make sure it's helpful to me.
I found a treasure chest in a tree.
I climbed the tree to try to get it.
Make sure it can fit.

Sarah Owen (8)
Ferrars Junior School, Luton

Fear

Fear is like cold, black blood running down my warm spine.
It smells like rotting flesh of a cow.
It sounds like a creaky door in a haunted mansion.
It tastes like sour milk stuck inside my throat.
It looks like a tall, dark shadow coming towards me.
It reminds me of death!

Arandeep Bains (11)
Ferrars Junior School, Luton

Anger

Anger is the colour red.
Anger tastes like sour lemons.
Anger sounds like my fast, speedy heartbeat.
Anger looks like a fierce volcano about to erupt.
Anger feels like you're going to do something really bad.
Anger is a pain you can't get rid of.

Joshua Hedley (11)
Ferrars Junior School, Luton

My Dream

I can taste the salty air,
I can feel my body in the water as I'm swimming.
Yet I can't see any water around me,
But I feel the sand on my feet as I'm walking.

I can hear the waves in the sea,
I see the salt dissolving as I pour it,
But the waves are miles away.
Yet I can't help myself gazing.

I can feel the soft sand on my feet,
I can feel the sun beaming down on the golden sand.
Yet I still feel cold inside,
While the warm, salty sea is splashing on me.

Muhammed Haque (10)
Ferrars Junior School, Luton

My Dream

I can smell the walnuts
On the fire, crackling.
Yet I can't see a cooker lit
And still no sign of them burning.

As you walk on the beach
You feel your feet stinging.
But there's no sun this winter,
Although every night I'm dreaming.

I can feel the heat
Running down my spine, melting.
Yet the icy white snow
Envelops my body, I'm freezing.

Hayley Fuller (10)
Ferrars Junior School, Luton

Seven Little Children

(Inspired by 'Ten Little Schoolboys' by A A Milne)

Seven little children,
Picking up sticks.
One got hurt,
And then there were six.

Six little children,
Learning to dive.
One got seasick,
And then there were five.

Five little children,
Opening the door.
One got hurt,
And then there were four.

Four little children,
Climbing a tree.
One fell down,
And then there were three.

Three little children,
Tying up their shoe.
One got stuck,
And then there were two.

Two little children,
Rubbing their tum.
One said, 'Yum,'
And then there was one.

One little child,
Going for a run.
He fell over,
And then there were none.

Jade Richards & Mollie Macdonald (8)
Ferrars Junior School, Luton

The Train Journey

A sobbing child was on a bustling platform,
Her face as white as snow,
With no family around her,
Clip-clop was all she could hear,
The crowd pushing and shoving,
Hurling the children into the train.

On the train,
London whizzing past,
Bang! Another bomb went off,
But she is still alive on the train,
The countryside catching up,
Her legs were wobbling like jelly.

Out of the train she went,
Her mind fixed upon the person she was staying with,
Suddenly a carriage showed up,
Her ride was there,
There were lots of children already waiting,
After the war she went back to London.

Hanifa Tidjani (9)
Ferrars Junior School, Luton

Travel

I can smell the candyfloss
On the candy maker.
Spinning around getting me sick,
I'm hoping I'm a baker.

I can hear the screams and laughter
Going up and down
On the roller coaster,
I can see a lot and downtown.

The sun blocking my eyes
But still feel chills down my spine.
I'm trying to get my money
And still got to pay my fine.

Emmanuel Gooding (9)
Ferrars Junior School, Luton

Sadness

Sadness is dark blue like the sea,
It sounds like the faint cry of a baby,
It reminds me of silence and tears,
It feels like my heart being ripped out,
It tastes like sour lemons,
It looks like a graveyard, quiet as a backstreet alley.

Mark Lomax (10)
Ferrars Junior School, Luton

Laughter

Laughter is as yellow as the daylight sun.
It sounds like the church choir singing.
It reminds me of strange, weird things.
It feels like the rain tickling me.
It smells like the autumn leaves falling from the trees.
It taste like sparkling water tingling its way down my throat.

Chloe Moore (10)
Ferrars Junior School, Luton

My Olympics Poem

Standing at the start waiting, waiting for the gun.
Will I win? I don't know.
My heart is pounding really fast.
My legs start to go slow but then I shout,
'Come on, let's go faster!'
Running, running, faster and faster.
I'm nearly there.
I come first.
I get my trophy on the podium,
Standing there really proud and tall.

Lauren Wood (8)
Flamstead End Primary School, Cheshunt

My Olympics Poem

Here I am waiting to hear the gun bang!
The gun went.
I was right at the back.
I was really scared I was going to lose,
But in a second I was back in the lead.
The finish line was only ten metres away.
Then I was coming back in the race,
Then I was in second place.
Five metres away, I was nearly in first place.
I couldn't believe it, I was first.
One metre to go, I came first.
My mum was cheering,
I won Olympic gold.

Harry Goodwin (8)
Flamstead End Primary School, Cheshunt

My Olympics Poem

I am waiting for the gun to bang!
I think I am going to win.
Bang! I'm starting.
Someone is in front,
Now I'm first.
I think I will win.
Round the trees I go,
The wind flying through my hair.
My mum is cheering all the way through.
I'm making zooming noises.
Whoo, I won,
I got the gold medal.

Amy Littleford (8)
Flamstead End Primary School, Cheshunt

My Olympics Poem

Waiting at the start till the guns go bang.
My heart's shivering, I'm going to lose.
I start to run,
I'm looking at the crowd.
I can't see my mum, what should I do?
Then I see my mum running in, getting the camera out.
There goes the flash of the digital camera.
I am still running, I'm second place,
Will I come first or will I lose?
One lap left.
I'm looking quite nervous.
I'm in first place.
I'm looking away.
I cross the line,
Am I first?
Yes, what a surprise.
Everyone's cheering at me.
I'm standing on the podium with my incredible medal.
I get down from the podium,
Oops I slipped, I've grazed my knees,
What should I do?

Rachel Banner (8)
Flamstead End Primary School, Cheshunt

My Olympics Poem

I'm waiting, I'm waiting for the race to begin,
I'm very scared, am I going to win?
The man blows his whistle, the race begins,
I'm winning, I'm winning, I'm going to win.
My heart is pounding very fast,
I won, I won, yes!
I stand on the podium, everybody's screaming,
I can't believe it, I must be dreaming.

Georginana Ioannou (8)
Flamstead End Primary School, Cheshunt

My Olympics Poem

I'm waiting for the race to start.
Boom! There goes the gun,
Everyone starts.
Where am I? Last or first?
Who knows?
I'm zooming past all the other racers.
I'm nearly there, in about 3 seconds.
Later I'm on the podium,
Everyone's cheering,
My heart is going bump, bump, bump.
I'm really proud,
I'm smiling to my ears,
Yippee I've won.

Alex Kiely (8)
Flamstead End Primary School, Cheshunt

My Olympics Poem

I'm waiting at the starting line,
I'm feeling very fine.

I'm standing very proud
With a very loud crowd.

Am I going to win? I don't know
I can be very slow.

I've come in first place
And bashed my face.

I'm standing on the podium happy and proud
And waving to the crowd.

Ben Parker (8)
Flamstead End Primary School, Cheshunt

My Olympics Poem

I'm standing, I'm standing, I'm standing at the line,
Please I have to beat their time.
I took the lead,
Then I tripped over a weed.
Don't worry I'm not there
But who cares, I've got my cuddly bear.

Alfie Merridale (8)
Flamstead End Primary School, Cheshunt

My Olympics Poem

I'm waiting, I'm waiting, for the race to begin.
My heart is pounding, I'm not going to win.
My heart is pounding, the gun goes *boom!*
I run, I run, then I zoom!
I pass the line, I scream and shout!
I'm definitely not the odd one out!

Vanessa Blair (8)
Flamstead End Primary School, Cheshunt

Cold Nights

Cold nights
When you warm your jumpers beside the fire
and the freezing rain pours
and the freezing breeze blows past all the cities
and all the fires burn and the roaring fires roar
and the snow pours.

Samuel Rowden (8)
Flamstead End Primary School, Cheshunt

My Olympics Poem

I'm getting ready for the race,
I'm getting nervous.

I'm standing there waiting for the gun.
The gun goes *bang!*
I go as fast as my legs can carry me.
I start to sweat.

My mum says, 'Run! Run!' but my legs slow down.
I say, 'Go legs go!'
I start, I start to go faster and faster
From the back to the front, I'm a second away from the finish.
The race is over.
Am I first, last? What place am I?

I stand on the podium with my medal.
It's a carat gold!

Daniel Key (8)
Flamstead End Primary School, Cheshunt

My Olympics Poem

I am crouching down and waiting for the red and white flag
                                      to go down.
Now it has gone.
I had better start running.
Off I go speeding from last to second.
The boy who is in front has won this race every year.
I don't stand a chance but I will carry on with the race.
We are coming near to the end.
Suddenly the boy falls over, I take the lead and I win the race.
The person who is responsible for the race comes
        and gives me a gold medal that says my name on it
And now I do a lot of Olympic races.

Melissa Howard (9)
Flamstead End Primary School, Cheshunt

My Olympics Poem

Standing and waiting for the race to start.
Standing there, watch me dart.
My mum cheering, 'Go all the way!'
And my baby sister says, 'Hooray!'
I'm halfway through the race,
Hopefully won't fall on my face.
I run past the finish line, I'm going to burst.
I hear my name, I've just come first.
I run up to my mum and give her a hug,
She goes in a bag and pulls out a mug.
My dad says, 'Well done.
Let's go and have some fun.'
Then the next race is starting,
I won't be darting.
I'm scared,
It's the end, I should be prepared.

Raynor Belloguet (9)
Flamstead End Primary School, Cheshunt

My Olympic Poem

I'm warming up for the race,
I am warming up in a slow and steady pace.
I'm standing on the line and I'm feeling fine.
I hear, 'Ready, steady, go!'
I run off the line quicker than you can say hello.
I'm halfway across the track, I can't give up now,
I'm running for my brother Mac.
I have broken the ribbon, I have come first.
I need to get a drink now, I'm dying of thirst.
I have got my medal, I feel proud.
I am so happy that I bend down and bow.

Brandon Fagan (9)
Flamstead End Primary School, Cheshunt

My Olympics Poem

Standing on the line until the gun goes *bang!*
Off we go,
Come on legs, away we go.
But I'm getting nervous though
So away we begin with me in 4th place.
I see a man beside me playing his base.

My heart is pounding, *boom! Boom! Boom!*
I have some sweat dripping from my head, I wipe it off.
My heart is still pumping
And my legs are still sprinting.

Finally I cross the line.
Where am I, 1st, 2nd, 3rd?
I stand on the podium proud and bold with a sparkling gold!

Kelsey Barron (9)
Flamstead End Primary School, Cheshunt

My Olympics Poem

I am running down the road.
I might be late . . .
Bam! Off goes the gun
So I start to run faster and faster,
As quick as my legs can carry me.
Suddenly I go in front.
'Whoopee,' screams my brother.
Then I start to crouch down low
Two more rounds, I'm nearly there.
My heart is pounding, it's gonna burst.
Everyone starts counting, '10, 9, 8, 7, 6, 5, 4, 3, 2, 1!'
Rip! There I go through the line
'Whoopee!' I scream
There I stand on the podium, my heart filled with pride!

India Wayland (9)
Flamstead End Primary School, Cheshunt

Winter So Cold

Cold, cold winter.
On the 25th December, it's Christmas.
Snow falls so cold.
You have snowball fights,
You build snowmen with a carrot nose.
Icicles hang from branches on the trees.
On the 24th December at night
Children are warm in their beds
Here comes Santa putting gifts under our tree
In December you decorate your house and trees
You bring gifts
It's freezing outside
It's a cold night, morning and afternoon.
On the last day of each year
Let's celebrate New Year tomorrow.

Courtney Chidgzey (8)
Flamstead End Primary School, Cheshunt

Christmas Time

Falling snowflakes in the air
calling Christmas so fair.

Children playing in the snow
throwing snowballs in the snow.

People pulling crackers, eating food,
playing and giving presents and toys.

Winter is going, summer is coming
so unwrap your presents
Christmas is going.

Huddle round the fire eating marshmallows on sticks.
Have a hot drink and eat treats.

Benn Lee (9)
Flamstead End Primary School, Cheshunt

Christmas Is Coming

Winter is coming.
Christmas is near.
We like presents and we are here.
Everyone will come.

Winter is cold and very chilly.
We don't want to get up.
The snow is falling.
We want to make snowmen.

Christmas Eve is here, we are having dinner.
We are having fun.
We want presents and love
Tomorrow is Christmas Day.

It's here! It's here!
We can open presents
It is the best
Christmas Day!

Amelia Diston (9)
Flamstead End Primary School, Cheshunt

Winter

Winter is here, it is bright and clear
with a little sparkle on the grass

The winter passes very fast
and all the snowmen don't last
and the festivals have passed
and all the leaves fall fast.

It gets dark early when the clocks go back
it's frosty in the morning and as I walk
I hear the ground crunch and crack.

Joe Hannigan (9)
Flamstead End Primary School, Cheshunt

A Very, Very Cold Night

A windy night, a windy night.
I don't know how it could be so bright.
Snow is falling, snow is falling.
I wish it would hurry up to the morning.
Thunder and lightning, thunder and lightning.
It is very, very frightening.
A windy night, a windy night.

A windy night, a windy night.
It is such a big fright.
Dress up warm, dress up warm,
To keep me away from the storm.
It's not sunny, it's not sunny
And I am very, very unhappy.
A windy night, a windy night.

Brandon Joy (8)
Flamstead End Primary School, Cheshunt

Winter Frost

When it is dark,
a dog might bark.

When the ground is full of snow,
be careful, the wind might blow.

Winter frost.

In winter you need hats and scarves,
but I don't think you'll hear any laughs.

Cosy houses,
people go to Brownies.

Lucy Carter-Vale (8)
Flamstead End Primary School, Cheshunt

Winter Fun

In winter it snows
In winter it glows.

And outside it is dark
And all the dogs bark.

All the robins come
And all the kids are having fun.

Christmas is on its way
And Santa's cleaning his sleigh.

Everyone's making snowmen
And the street lights look like glowing men.

And the people are putting lights up
And adults hold hot cups.

Lara Gamby (8)
Flamstead End Primary School, Cheshunt

One Cold Winter Day

One cold winter day
I put on my coat
and went out to play

When I went outside
I saw my friend,
'Are you OK?'

I went into the warm
and rested my head.

Winter is nice
but cold as ice
and bitter outside.

Sarah Winter
Flamstead End Primary School, Cheshunt

Winter Is Here

In winter I wrap up in warm pyjamas,
In the day I like to eat bananas.

In winter it is bitter,
There is lots of litter.

Christmas is on its way,
And Santa is cleaning his sleigh.

The robins come,
Even adults are having fun.

The night is dark,
The dogs bark.

All the cars are covered in snow,
All the houses glow.

Rebecca Dawson (9)
Flamstead End Primary School, Cheshunt

Frosty Nights

Winter is cold
Frosty nights and mornings
Rain and fog
Frosty nights and rain

Rain and frost on the cars and vans
Eat your cherry pie now
Happy Christmas Day
Frosty houses, keep the fire burning over Christmas Day
Ho! Ho! Ho!

Jack Rowden (8)
Flamstead End Primary School, Cheshunt

Winter Nights

As it gets dark
In winter lots of dogs bark
In winter cars get blocked
You might want to put on your socks
In winter you might slip
You want some tea? Do you want a sip?
In winter you throw snowballs
Lucky in your house you have walls
In winter you get stuck in the snow
And people will get angry from the snowballs that you throw.

Chloe Richards (8)
Flamstead End Primary School, Cheshunt

Winter Poem

Cold and frosty nights
Sitting in front of the fire
Just got out of the bath
Putting warm pyjamas on
It's going to snow tonight
Or is it going to rain?
Christmas is coming
I love Christmas.

Harry Richardson (8)
Flamstead End Primary School, Cheshunt

Winter Comes, Winter Goes

Frost and snow
Children with hats and scarves and warm jumpers
Dark cold nights and rain
And people in their cosy houses by the roaring fire
Now it is not winter anymore,
Now it's spring, bye-bye.

Jay Barlow (8)
Flamstead End Primary School, Cheshunt

Ho! Ho! Ho!

Ho! Ho! Ho! It's Christmas,
Wintertime is here
Snowflakes falling to the ground,
We all let out a cheer,
We put our coats and hats on,
We all go out to play,
We make a great big snowman,
And hope he's here to stay.
We love it when it's winter,
Mr Frosty on the ground,
He lies so still and silent,
Not making any sound.

Aaron Elliott (9)
Flamstead End Primary School, Cheshunt

Winter Times

Frosty nights, cold days
Snow is not as warm as the warm hay
You have a cocoa
And see Santa, 'Ho, ho, ho!'
I'm a bit perky today
I'm having a turkey today
Feel the breeze
But you might freeze
You open your presents
You look for pheasants.

Benjamin Howell (9)
Flamstead End Primary School, Cheshunt

Ten Schoolchildren

(Inspired by 'Ten Little Schoolboys' by A A Milne)

Ten schoolchildren standing in a line,
One walked out, then there were nine.

Nine schoolchildren standing at the gate,
One walked through, then there were eight.

Eight schoolchildren standing in Heaven,
One went to Devon, then there were seven.

Seven schoolchildren standing in a line,
One needed to be fixed, then there were six.

Six schoolchildren standing in a line,
One wasn't too alive, then there were five.

Five schoolchildren standing in a line,
One was very poor, then there were four.

Four schoolchildren standing in a line,
One wasn't with me, then there were three.

Three schoolchildren standing in a line,
One needed the loo, then there were two.

Two schoolchildren standing in a line,
One wanted a bun, then there was one.

One schoolchild standing in a line,
He was the only one, then there were none.

Erin Thackeray (7)
Gaddesden Row JMI School, Hemel Hempstead

Ten Mums

(Inspired by 'Ten Little Schoolboys' by A A Milne)

Ten mums standing in a line,
One went home, so there were nine.

Nine mums and one was late,
Did not come back so then there were eight.

Eight mums but one went to Devon,
She stayed there and then there were seven.

Seven mums but one played some tricks,
Broke her leg and then there were six.

Six mums but one took a dive,
Went to sleep so then there were five.

Five mums, one won a door,
She took forever and then there were four.

Four mums, one got killed by a bee,
And so then there were three.

Three mums, one lost a shoe,
Went to find it and then there were two.

Two mums, one was hit on the bum,
It was sore so then there was one.

One mum had no fun!
Went home and then there were none!

Aylwen Hadley (8)
Gaddesden Row JMI School, Hemel Hempstead

Ten School Dinner Ladies

(Inspired by 'Ten Little Schoolboys' by A A Milne)

Ten school dinner ladies,
Feeding children in the line,
One got blown away and then there were nine.

Nine school dinner ladies,
They came to school late,
One got hypnotised and then there were eight.

Eight school dinner ladies,
But one went to Devon,
She decided to live there and then there were seven.

Seven school dinner ladies,
Serving slugs and sticks,
One exploded and then there were six.

Six school dinner ladies,
One had a baby called Clive,
And she had to stay with him and then there were five.

Five school dinner ladies,
Climbing through the door,
One got locked out and then there were four.

Four school dinner ladies,
But one lost the key,
So she couldn't get into school and then there were three.

Three school dinner ladies,
But one lost her shoe,
And her sock caught on fire and then there were two.

Two school dinner ladies,
Cursing children's fun,
One was kidnapped and then there was one.

One school dinner lady,
Standing alone in the sun,
The children attacked her and then there were none.

Lucy Hodson (8)
Gaddesden Row JMI School, Hemel Hempstead

Ten Arsenal Footballers

(Inspired by 'Ten Little Schoolboys' by A A Milne)

Ten Arsenal footballers all looking fine,
One got shot, then there were nine.

Nine Arsenal footballers being used as bait,
One was eaten and then there were eight.

Eight Arsenal footballers going to Devon,
One got stuck in quicksand and then there were seven.

Seven Arsenal footballers eating some Twix,
One had poison in it and then there were six.

Six Arsenal footballers ready to dive,
One fell in and broke his head and then there were five.

Five Arsenal footballers gluing the floor,
One got glued up, and then there were four.

Four Arsenal footballers going to ski,
One got tangled up and then there were three.

Three Arsenal footballers all shouting, 'Boo!'
One got hit by a stone and then there were two.

Two Arsenal footballers going to see their mum,
One got kicked and then there was one!

One Arsenal footballer being a hero,
He fell off a roof and then there were *none!*

Conor Grant (8)
Gaddesden Row JMI School, Hemel Hempstead

Football Crazy

Football has loads of tricks,
Always deflecting off big bricks.

Stadiums built all year round,
So they can fit in an awesome crowd.

David Beckham came out the door,
Tripped over his laces and fell on the floor.

Wayne Rooney tried to shoot,
Then slipped and lost his boot.
He stubbed his toe
And shouted, 'Oh no.'

The weather was mild,
But the crowd was still wild.

Thierry Henry shouted, 'That ball's mine,'
Scored and gave his team the winning scoreline.

Jamie Henderson (9)
Garden Fields JMI School, St Albans

Elephants

Elephants, elephants, they are great,
They have large tusks
That are hard to break.

Elephants, elephants, have big ears,
They walk along and have no fear.

Elephants, elephants, have big feet,
They walk quite slow
Because of the heat.

Elephants, elephants, blink their eyes,
It is because of the flies.

Chrystal Smith (8)
Garden Fields JMI School, St Albans

If I Were A Giraffe

If I were a giraffe,
I would have such a laugh.
Walking around munching trees all day,
Then I would go off and play.
I'd use my long black tongue to eat my food,
I don't wear clothes, I'm always in the nude!
Using my beautiful patterns to attract the guys
And my hair and tail to swat away the flies!
To drink water, I'd have to bend down far,
If I was playing golf, I'd get at least a par!
With my neck so tall, I'm in the clouds,
Standing up, tall and proud.
Yellow and brown, lucky me,
I'm not dangerous, as you can see!

Louise Anstee (11)
Garden Fields JMI School, St Albans

Jasmin

Black all over and covered in fur,
She has green eyes and likes to purr.
She isn't too tall and she's quite small,
Outside she likes to pounce and catch a little mouse.
She has two sisters, Tabby and Jess,
Sometimes they can be pests!
They climb up the curtains,
That's not good, for certain.
Jasmin's my cat, good as gold,
Always does what she's told . . .

Not!

Joanne Anstee (8)
Garden Fields JMI School, St Albans

The Toilet Seat Has Teeth

The bathroom has gone crazy, far beyond belief.
The sink is full of spiders
And the toilet seat has teeth.

The plughole in the bath
Has a whirlpool underneath
That pulls you down feet first
And the toilet seat has teeth.

The toothpaste tube is purple
And makes your teeth fall out,
The toilet roll is nettles
And makes you scream and shout!

The towels have got bristles
As the bubblebath is glue.
The soap has turned into jelly
And it makes your skin bright blue.

The hot tap gushes forth with sludge
That is bright pink,
The cold tap dribbles lumps of green
That block the sink.

The mirror's pulling faces at everyone it can,
The shower's dripping marmalade
And blackcurrant jam.

The rubber ducks are breeding
And building their own nests
With shaving foam and tissues
In Grandad's stringy vest.

Shampoo is liquid dynamite
There's petrol in the hairspray
Both will cure dandruff
When they blow your head away.

The bathroom has gone crazy, far beyond belief,
The sink is full of spiders
And the toilet seat has teeth.

Pritish Chauhan (11)
Garden Fields JMI School, St Albans

My Magical Teddy Bear

My teddy bear's called Lattee.
My teddy bear goes everywhere!
When we go to school I leave him on the stair
But he jumps up and doesn't take good care.
He goes on adventures but forgets about the time,
We can't find him, he's definitely not home,
He's gone out all alone!
My other teddy bears are there
Exactly where I left them
But where's my teddy bear Lattee?
My other teddy bears know
He's gone to karate!
He loves karate but he loves me more,
I'm sure he didn't mean to upset me.
But at karate someone hit his knee,
He can't get home all night,
He sits on a stone till morning light.
I have to do without him,
But the next day he's not away,
He's back in my bed
Being my ted as usual!

Rosalind Bennett (8)
Garden Fields JMI School, St Albans

Best Friends

They're always there for you.
Sometimes funny too.
Always happy when you achieve things.
What could you do without a friend?
Funny, happy, always brightens up your day.
Without a friend I would be sunk.
Make a new friend, be happy, be funny, make your day really fun.

Lauren Hart & Freya McCann (9)
Garden Fields JMI School, St Albans

The Creeper

One look at the creeper will fill you with awe,
His mouth is a cavern, a vice is his jaw.

His girth is prodigious, the kind you acquire,
When appetite burns like a forest on fire.

His teeth are an arsenal of blades and machetes
With power enough for dismembering yetis.

His gut is a cess pool of juices corrosive
And poisonous acid and gases explosive.

His throat is like a drainpipe, will carry you down
In a river of mucus you'll struggle, then drown.

His bowel a dungeon, a pit of despair
And all those that enter will perish in there.

He'll lure you with cunning, beguile you with lies,
But whatever you do, don't look into his eyes.

They are swollen with evil, distended with malice
His motives are wicked, his methods are callous.

For this is the creeper, he'll fill you with awe,
His mouth is a cavern, a vice is his jaw.

Vikesh Chauhan (8)
Garden Fields JMI School, St Albans

Detention

I've got three black spots.
Now I'm in detention.
Why do we have detention?
It's just sitting down doing lines at playtime.
Is it to keep us quiet
Or to keep us from having fun?
Mummy says, 'Be good and don't get black spots.'
How do you not get black spots?
It's not fair, everyone else can.

The teachers seem so angry when we talk.
They shout at us to *shut up!*
Then if we do it again they just say . . .
'Black spot! See you after school.'
It's just a nightmare.
Everyone says I'm really, really, really naughty.
I am proud to say I'm the naughtiest in the school.
Imagine that.
I can't remember any kind thing that any teacher has said to me.
Teachers hate me, but I don't care.

Uh-oh, the teacher has just realised what I am doing.
This is going to be serious, well - more than serious.
The teacher is red in the face and walking towards me.
Ouch! He is pulling my ear, pinching hard.
Dear, dear, he's thrown me out of the door.
Guess what he's saying -
'Be suspended and have another . . .
Detention!'

Grace Pitkethly (9)
Gresham's Preparatory School, Holt

The Frosty Planet

If I were queen of the Frosty Planet,
Where it's as cold as a freezer.
It would be so relaxing.
Gazing at the picture, I see frost fur,
Rustling, crisping as they start to stroll.
The fresh white snow is a mass of footprints,
Now they are dancing,
Jumping to the moon.

I start to munch,
My hand is deep down,
Rattle, crunch!
Snow slips through my icy fingers,
I run towards them.
The polar bears skip about and celebrate,
Because I am the only queen of the Frosty Planet.

But only until tomorrow,
When the golden sun will open its huge red mouth
And shine through my window.

Layla Myers (9)
Gresham's Preparatory School, Holt

Tiger Picture Poem

(After 'Tiger in a Tropical Storm' painted by Henri Rousseau)

His eyes sparkled like the night stars.
His tough, terrifying teeth chattered.
Sharp, razor-like claws clutched the grass.
His swishing tail whipped along his back.
His wet, soggy nose twitched with anticipation.
The wind whistled in his pricked-up ears.
His legs stretched like elastic.
His back arched like a bridge.

The lightning came down.
Eerie, eroding tree trunks tilted over.
Crunch.
Snap.
The grass wilted.
The tropical plants chatted amongst themselves.
The stormy sky darkened, like a computer turning off.
The breathing of the tiger slowed, he was ready.
Ready for his prey.

Alice Hare (9)
Gresham's Preparatory School, Holt

Dartmoor

If I were the Lord of Dartmoor,
And my land was as yellow as the sun,
Happiness is everywhere, there in my little land.

Gazing at the picture, I feel
The green grass tickling my feet.
Whoosh! the wind through my hair.
Tweet! go the birds up high.
The grass and trees would bow down to me,
All my world would come to meet me.
My world would be happy.

Staring through my window,
I see a mud track trailing off.
The hills, as beautiful as ever.
The sky is turquoise blue.
Every day the sun jumps out of bed,
And strokes my world, to raise its head.

Jack Barter (10)
Gresham's Preparatory School, Holt

Sugar City

If I were the lord of Sugar City . . .
The sugar would be as sweet as honey,
The silver-whiteness would dazzle me.
Hunger would haunt me.
Slurp - I would taste the marvellous sugar.
Crunch - it would be so delicious.
I would see sugar ants walking into sugar shops,
Marching up sugar mountains.
It would be a beautiful city.

If I were the lord of Sugar City . . .
The sugar ants would troop,
Blowing trumpets when they got to the top.
They'd call, 'Attack!' to the other ants.
The sugar cubes would tremble as the ants attacked,
Tumbling down, down, down into blackness.
The ants would disappear with the sugar.
I'd wonder as I sprinkled sugar into my tea.

Clare Mawson (9)
Gresham's Preparatory School, Holt

Fun Land

If I were Lord of Fun Land I would see . . .
The Gyrocopter, like a bee, taking people for a ride.
Happiness is humming in the bright sky.
Gazing at the picture, jolly Gyro gliding round
Whizzing,
It soars around the sky,
Yellow and black,
Full of tranquillity.

If I were Lord of Fun Land
I would get jolly Gyro to pick me up for a ride.
Sting.
An army of wasps invades,
He flings me down and goes
Weaving through the wasps, shouting,
'Die! Die! Die!'
His voice fades . . .

Gregor Bailey (9)
Gresham's Preparatory School, Holt

Treeland

If I were the lord of trees,
The snow as white as milk,
Happiness is everywhere, happiness is good.
Gazing at the picture, the mini mountains migrate,
Slam! A brick falls, *Crash!* Another one.
The snow sleeps on the ground.
I look up but can see nothing,
For the snow is getting thick.

The church bells chime fiercely,
It is so loud, the snow on the houses quivers.
The birds squawk.
The birds fly away with their graceful black wings.
They land on a snowy roof.
Far away, the world begins to thaw.

Karina Olsen (9)
Gresham's Preparatory School, Holt

The Three Little Pigs

The poor pigs were so big.
None felt like doing a piggy-jig.

The first pig brought straw, nicely cut,
And built himself a little hut.

Wolfie came and licked his lips,
And stood there gleaming, stretching his hips.

The wolf just stood and blew and blew,
Piggie stood and said, 'Oh pooh! Boohoo!'

Poor Piggie lay all fat and dead,
Upon his hot frying pan bed.

The wolf was not full up yet,
He'll find another one, I bet!

Second piggie's house was going well
The wolf came along, the pig thought *hell!*

The pig got stressed, he would die,
Oh no, oh yes! He's in a pie.

Oh golly, oh gosh you are right
He's in Wolfie's tummy, nice and tight.

The final pig was good and brave,
He had a brick house, not a cave.

The pig was so great and thoughtful,
Oh yes that pig was so beautiful.

The wolf came down the chimney hot,
And fell in *splash!* to a boiling pot.

The third pig had defeated the one and only
Wolf, who is now living very gloomily.

This pig was a happy Jack,
But watch out Jack, he'll be back!

But Jack and the Beanstalk
Is another story.

Harriet Shaw (8)
Gresham's Preparatory School, Holt

Best Friends Forever

If I were a lady of companionship,
Friendship would be as solid as a rock.
As important as life,
Gazing at the picture, the gentle graceful girls grin,
They chuckle and rustle their yellow toys,
Dressed almost identically in white frills,
Preparing a tea party for the discarded dollies.

The two girls each in their own worlds,
Shoulder to shoulder,
Quiet as mice,
As I watch my mum,
With her finger on the picture,
A tear d
r
o
p
s
Down her melancholy cheek.

Caitlin Astley (9)
Gresham's Preparatory School, Holt

Hope

If I were lord of the land of Hope -
The sky would be as blue as the ocean.
The mystical moon would shine.
Gazing at the picture I would see a smooth sunset
                                    shimmering over the land.
The bushes would rustle as a bird flew over the moon,
                                    tweeting as it soared.
The trees of green would be so smooth.
The cat's eyes would glitter in the gloom
And the breeze would drift around.

If I were lord of the land of Hope
The moon would be an eye gazing upon me.
A hooting sound would echo around, bouncing off the walls.
The chapel door would creak open as if beckoning me in.
The silence would feel spiritual as darkness descended.
Moonlight would stretch across the land.
The stained-glass window would be as colourful as a rainbow
And the moon would disappear as the colour turned austere.

Abbie Glover (9)
Gresham's Preparatory School, Holt

Fluff And Puff

If I were lord of Fluff and Puff
The different colour fur like stormy clouds,
Bouncing on the fluff - cosiness all round.
Gazing at the picture, a bird bouncing on the fluff,
The tortoiseshell fur as soft as a cushion.
The white clouds moved swiftly through the air.
I had stolen the clouds.

Puff was letting out the hot air in my face like fresh breath.
The peppermint taste was spicy, hot yet peaceful.
Gazing at the picture, all I could see was the fog from
                                        people breathing.
Blow - the breath swept me off my feet.
The red-hot tonsils took me somewhere.
I had taken the breeze, there was none left.
The concrete heaved when I puffed in.
It was bouncing, bouncing - until everything had gone.

Florence Baldwin (9)
Gresham's Preparatory School, Holt

Gleedis

If I were lord of Gleedis -
Happiness would be as bright as the sun.
Nostalgia would be a really long bit of string.
Gazing at the picture, I would see a far-off family giggling at me.
The smell of the wind would dazzle me and the lion's roar
would hurt me.
The hills would be like huge boulders looking down at me.

If I were lord of Gleedis -
The darkness would close around me,
All I would hear would be the laughter from the far-off family.
As the camera opened its eyes on the children, I would see
them chit-chatting.
Jolly James and Laughing Luke would look at me with an expression
of happiness on their faces.

At last I would be touched.
It would always be there for me.

Conrad Redmayne (10)
Gresham's Preparatory School, Holt

My Anger Poem

Anger is like burning sausages,
Anger is like black or red,
Anger is like reminding me of me,
Anger is like a very black bird,
Anger is like a very black blackboard,
Anger is like a bird tweeting for help
And the smell of burning.

Miranda Skeats (8)
Greyfriars Primary School, King's Lynn

Embarrassment

Embarrassment is like the colour
of the most scarlet red in the world.

Embarrassment is like the most powerful
smell of roses.

Embarrassment sounds like millions of
people laughing.

Embarrassment tastes like the sweetest
taste ever.

Embarrassment looks like magenta-red
roses.

Embarrassment reminds me of my friends.

Kourtney Hitchcock (10)
Greyfriars Primary School, King's Lynn

Anger

Anger is like a blackboard after the cleaner
has wiped it with a wet cloth.

Anger is like a drum beating the same rhythm
again and again.

Anger in my mind is like an exploding star.

Anger feels like thorns pressing into your skin
and forcing out blood.

Anger tastes like a red-hot chilli pepper
burning your mouth.

Anger reminds me of a thousand knives
stabbing me and tearing me up.

Kodiey Yallop (11)
Greyfriars Primary School, King's Lynn

Fun

Fun is red like a very soft heart.
Fun makes everybody enjoy, like me.
It tastes like a heart sweet.
Fun smells like a love heart.
It looks like a rainbow,
It feels like a fish.
It reminds me of the end.

Sabrina Hichcock (8)
Greyfriars Primary School, King's Lynn

Sadness

Sadness is blue
Like the sea and tears are like the waves in the sea
It feels cold and hurtful
It smells like the salty sea
It looks like the sea dripping off a person
It sounds like me when I am crying
It's remembering my brother
It tastes horrible.

Megan Watson (7)
Greyfriars Primary School, King's Lynn

Hate

Hate is black like darkness,
It sounds like anger,
It tastes like blackberry pie,
It smells like an evil devil,
It looks like a dragon,
It feels like slimy goo,
It reminds me of a black knight.

Harry Twyman (8)
Greyfriars Primary School, King's Lynn

Silence

Silence is grey like the end of the world.
Silence sounds like this and I hate it.
Silence tastes like disgusting spinach.
Silence smells like nice fresh air.
Silence looks like a light blue sky.
Silence feels like the wind blowing on you.
When silence is in you can hear a pin drop.
Being all alone is the worst thing ever.
I wish I had a brother or sister.
But silence reminds me of something nice . . .
The sea.

Callum Flynn Wallace (9)
Greyfriars Primary School, King's Lynn

Darkness

Darkness is brown like the tiles on the roof.
Darkness is black like the dark night sky.
Darkness is blue like the deep blue sea.
It looks like a really dark room.
It sounds like a spooky ghost going past.
It reminds me of a scary spider.
It smells like some stinky dog poo.
It tastes like some yucky dust.
It feels very scary.

Stewart Scott (7)
Greyfriars Primary School, King's Lynn

Fun

Fun is silvery gold like a shining medal.
It reminds me of my 7th birthday.
It sounds like 10,000 kids laughing at the same time.
It smells like a ton of chocolate being melted.
It looks like a hundred bunny rabbits in a flowery field.

Louis Morrish (8)
Greyfriars Primary School, King's Lynn

Anger

Anger is as real as pure blood from a fallen victim.
Anger sounds like a roar of fire burning through a building.
Anger looks like someone in pain, who has been shot by a gun.
Anger is as spicy as a deluxe chilli, hot spicy bean sauce.
Anger smells like rotten eggs, scrambled together.
Anger feels like a rough surface trying to burst out of the ground.
Anger reminds me of death.

Elvin Cheung (10)
Greyfriars Primary School, King's Lynn

Happiness

Happiness is as white as the sparkling stars.
Happiness smells as good as a thousand perfumes.
Happiness looks as beautiful as the most beautiful butterfly.
Happiness feels as soft as the softest feather.
Happiness sounds as sweet as any hummingbird.
Happiness tastes as ripe as the ripest red apple.
Happiness reminds me of my family and how much they love me.

Ryan Lee Reeve (10)
Greyfriars Primary School, King's Lynn

Rudeness

As green as the grass at summertime.
As sick as staring at a toad, when I stand near a pond.
As horrible as walking through doggy-doo.
It sounds as silly as hearing someone make silly noises.
It smells as weird as smelling a roast potato in the kitchen.
It tastes as gross as eating vegetables.
It reminds me of something very disgusting.

Chloe Ellis (9)
Greyfriars Primary School, King's Lynn

Sadness

Sadness is as loud as a million babies crying.
It feels like your mum and dad splitting up, when you don't know.
Sadness is the colour of a grey elephant stomping in the jungle.
It smells of lemon juice sitting on your lip, not coming off.
Sadness tastes as bitter as the wind blowing in your face.
It looks like people being killed secretly at night.
Sadness reminds you of people who have no money,
                                        living on the street.

Jessica Hill (9)
Greyfriars Primary School, King's Lynn

Sadness

Sadness feels like I am annoyed,
Sadness sounds like my heart is destroyed.
Sadness is as black as the sky at night,
Sadness looks like my dad had a fight.
Sadness tastes like a dropped dead rose,
Sadness smells like a couple of dead crows.
Sadness reminds me of a dark place.

Bexley Loose (9)
Greyfriars Primary School, King's Lynn

Happiness

Happiness is the colour blue.
Happiness tastes like chocolate gateau.
Happiness gives off the wonderful smell of vanilla essence.
Happiness is the sound of angels singing.
Happiness looks like a wrapped up present on Christmas Day.
Happiness feels like having a massage.
Happiness reminds me of winning a million pounds.

Jamie Hall (10)
Greyfriars Primary School, King's Lynn

Fear

Fear is as white as a snowy ghost,
Swaying from side to side, on the cold and misty coast.

Fear looks like a blank page with a black dot
And it is getting bigger, but you can't move, you're stuck to the spot.

Fear tastes like freezing metal, getting bigger in your mouth,
Like it's travelled all over the world - north, west, east and south.

Fear feels like a block of ice, melting on and on,
A smooth slippery surface and then in a while it's gone.

Fear reminds me of a blanket of silver snow on the ground,
Or maybe a frozen duck pond - no ducks, not a sound.

Lucy Barnes (10)
Greyfriars Primary School, King's Lynn

Angry

Angry because I have to tidy my room.
Angry like an unhappy baboon.
Angry when I have to go to school.
Angry when I break the rules.
Angry like a midnight storm.
Angry when I break a window.

Tadas Frieturminkas (11)
Greyfriars Primary School, King's Lynn

Spitefulness

It has the taste of a sour lemon.
It looks worse than a dead flower.
The colour of it is dark purple and black.
It sounds of thunder when it goes *crack.*
It feels really sharp and smells like burnt jam tarts.
It reminds me of a storm, over the sea.

Caitlin Nolan (10)
Greyfriars Primary School, King's Lynn

Happiness

Happiness is yellow like the big beautiful sun,
It tastes like chocolate melting on your tongue.
It smells like roses in the garden.
Happiness sounds like birds tweeting on the garden wall.
The grass is swaying as the wind rushes through it.
Happiness looks like a bunch of smiley faces.
It feels like your auntie giving you a big hug.
Happiness reminds me of memories that
I never want to forget.

Cara Hawes (8)
Greyfriars Primary School, King's Lynn

Hate

Hate is black like the darkness of the night.
Hate smells like the death of a loved one.
Hate sounds like thunder striking the ground.
Hate tastes like gravel and rock.
Hate looks like overwhelming darkness - you cannot escape it.
Hate feels like a thorn that cuts your hand.
It reminds me of death.

Dylan Goodfellow (9)
Greyfriars Primary School, King's Lynn

Anger

Anger is grey like a whirling tornado.
Anger sounds like a mighty dragon chomping.
Anger tastes like a huge black rock going down my throat.
Anger looks like a massive fire.
Anger feels very scary.
Anger reminds me of lizards.

Thomas Steward (7)
Greyfriars Primary School, King's Lynn

Sadness

Sadness is black like my own backpack.
It looks like my cat, who is very fat.
It feels so bad inside my mind.
It smells so bad, I can't understand what it would do to me.
It looks gruesome, dull and not nice.
It tastes like an out-of-date lollipop.
It reminds me of an old friend.

Sophie-Louise Nolan (8)
Greyfriars Primary School, King's Lynn

Hunger

It sounds like a rumbling rock
It tastes like disgusting spinach
It smells like a banana
It looks like a rumbling rock
It feels like race cars
It reminds me of Mars bars
The colour of it is brown.

Roy Black (8)
Greyfriars Primary School, King's Lynn

Sadness

Sadness is blue
Sadness tastes of the deep blue sea
Sadness is woe
Sadness is me
Sadness can be lifted with thoughts of happiness
So please don't think of sadness
Think of something else. Like me.

Harrie Reed (7)
Greyfriars Primary School, King's Lynn

Silence

Silence is like a blue clear sky on a summer's day.
Silence sounds like birds singing in the trees in the sunset.
Silence reminds me of me going on holiday to Spain,
                              where it was really hot.
Silence is like snow in layers, like a soft carpet, but cold.
Silence tastes like ice cream melting in your mouth. Yum-yum!
Silence feels like a smooth, soft pillow.
Silence smells like a gorgeous, lovely pizza.

Chloe Wigg (8)
Greyfriars Primary School, King's Lynn

Anger

Anger is red like a phoenix,
It tastes like boiling hot fire,
It feels like hard bumpy rock,
It smells like rotten old garbage,
It looks like a mighty magic dragon,
It reminds me of really hot chillies,
It sounds like a loud gorilla,
It makes me feel really angry.

Ben Austin (9)
Greyfriars Primary School, King's Lynn

Silence

Silence is golden like the rays of the sun.
It feels like a hot summer's day.
It looks like an ice cream.
It smells like your favourite food.
It sounds like the sea breeze.
It feels like a melted ice cream . . .
And it reminds me of peace.

Jacob Emerson (8)
Greyfriars Primary School, King's Lynn

Laughter

It looks like yellow sun,
It feels like a hyena,
It reminds me of my mum,
She jokes and makes me laugh all the time.
It sounds like a cheeky monkey, laughing all day long.
It tastes like water going down my throat, very fast.
It doesn't smell like anything.

Melissa Skeats (8)
Greyfriars Primary School, King's Lynn

Fear

Fear is dark like rain and darkness.
Fear is scary and frightening like death.
It feels like a red-hot volcano.
It tastes like cold freezing water.
It smells like a windy cold night.
It looks like a scary wolf barking.
It reminds me of when I was thunder storming.
It sounds like a buzzing bee.

Alison Sanpher (8)
Greyfriars Primary School, King's Lynn

Love

Love makes me cute
Love makes me cuddly
Love makes me happy
Love makes me a genius
Love makes me eat pizza.

Ben Wright (8)
Greyfriars Primary School, King's Lynn

Laugher

Laughter is orange like an orange crayon
It looks like a lion's mane,
It smells like a clean Great Dane.
Laughter tastes like carrots dipped in humus,
It spreads around like rumours.
It sounds like a man after a joke,
It feels like a small sponge.

Christopher Pavey (8)
Greyfriars Primary School, King's Lynn

Love Is Untouchable

Love is red like the bright red sunset,
Love looks like a red, red rose planted in my garden.
Love sounds like bluebirds chirping when the sun rises,
Love tastes like the yummy Loveheart chocolates.
Love feels like the smooth laundered clothes that I wear in the morning.
Love smells like the roses in my garden,
Love reminds me of my cat, licking her babies, getting them clean.

Lauren Gillies (9)
Greyfriars Primary School, King's Lynn

Happiness

Happiness is white like a rose, freshly picked.
It feels like wet bubble bath, that was made by a cat.
It tastes like a roast dinner, with French fries and pizza.
It reminds me of God and Jesus.
It sounds like a butterfly fluttering in the midday sun.
It smells like a sweet-pea sunbathing in the rays of the sun.
It looks like a bunch of moonlight fairies.
It makes me feel safe.

Thea Joslin (8)
Greyfriars Primary School, King's Lynn

The Lion

Roar! went the lion,
His teeth so sharp.
His claws outstretched.
His large eyes staring at his lunch.

Roar! went the lion.
His large body creeping quietly.
His paws ready to pounce.
His heart was beating fast.

Roar! went the lion.
His powerful legs chasing.
His prey was running, then
His tummy was full.

Kyle Rhys Hitchcock (7)
Greyfriars Primary School, King's Lynn

Hunger

Hunger is brown
Hunger is like lightning, smashing into a rock.
Yellow sparks come out of the lightning crash . . .
    Crash . . .
        Crash . . .
Sounds like a huge wave crashing into a city,
Tastes like rotten eggs,
Smells like a pig,
Looks like an evil devil,
Feels like a slimy snake,
Reminds me of a giant spider.

Elliot Holland (8)
Greyfriars Primary School, King's Lynn

My Pet Lucky

My pet Lucky
Is so bright
Jumping around
Like a wild kite.

My pet Lucky
Is so fluffy,
He makes me laugh,
Because he's so nutty.

My pet Lucky,
Sleeps all day,
But when I get home,
He just wants to play.

I love my pet Lucky,
And he loves me too.
Because we are best friends,
And I wanted you to know.

Georgia Kendall (9)
Gunthorpe School, Peterborough

Sharks

S harks are fierce, they are big
H ow do they live with other fish?
A t the surface eating fish,
R azor-sharp teeth,
K ing of the seas.
S harks are the best.

Matthew Baldwin (9)
Gunthorpe School, Peterborough

The Earth

The Earth spins around,
But it does not go down.
It does not make a sound
Going near the sun is out of bounds.

The Earth spins around,
And does not make a sound.

The Earth is near the sun,
The Earth is not a gun,
The Earth doesn't have a son,
The Earth isn't done.

The Earth spins around
And does not make a sound.

The Earth doesn't grow,
The Earth knows,
It goes
Around the sun.

The Earth spins around,
But it does not go down.
It does not make a sound,
Going near the sun is out of bounds.

The Earth spins around
But does not make a sound.

Paige Johnston (9)
Gunthorpe School, Peterborough

Mr Unsworth

Our teacher wasn't half as nice
as yours seems to be.

His name was Mr Unsworth
he taught us history.

And when you didn't know a date,
he'd get you by the ear.

And twist and twist and twist,
until it popped off.

Now let us praise the teachers
that are fine.

Make sure they don't draw
the line!

So we know teachers are worth the price,
because they're totally nice.

Connor Penson (10)
Gunthorpe School, Peterborough

My House Is A Zoo

My house is a zoo!
I've got a cat,
that is fat,
like a desert rat.

My house is a zoo!
I've got a hamster
that is brand new.

My house is a zoo!
I've got fishes
that do yellow poo.

My house is a zoo!
I've got stick insects,
we started with two
and ended up with more than a few.

Samantha Setchfield (9)
Gunthorpe School, Peterborough

The Monster From The Sun

He throws balls of fire,
He comes from the sun.
He's made of lava,
He always spoils your fun.

He's coming down to kill us,
He's so ugly, you would vomit.
Now he's coming down
Riding on a comet.

The person from the army,
With his gun of power.
Found the perfect aiming,
In less than an hour.

The monster dodged the rocket,
With incredible ease.
Then the monster fired back
With a flaming sneeze.

They made a giant cannon,
They knew some day they'd deploy it.
They aimed it at the monster,
And easily destroyed it.

Thomas Croote (9)
Gunthorpe School, Peterborough

Winter Morning

Winter is the king of the showmen,
Turning tree stumps into snowmen
And houses into birthday cakes
And spreading sugar over the lakes.
The world looks good enough to bite,
This is the season to be young,
Catching snowflakes on your tongue.

Jade Rossell (10)
Gunthorpe School, Peterborough

Summer Poem

Summer is coming
Summer is coming,
What can be better than
Summer coming?
We can splash, splash, splash
In the pool, getting people
Wet, wet, wet.

Summer is coming,
Summer is coming.
What could be better than
Hot, tanning weather?

We can, can, can have water fights,
To get our friends
Wet, wet, wet.

Summer is coming,
Summer is coming,
Yippee, we can play
In the hot, hot, hot weather.

Laura Kohter (10)
Gunthorpe School, Peterborough

Out Time - In Time

Out time, out time
teachers always
shout time!
In time, in time
teachers always
grin time.
Out time, out time
pets are all about time
In time, in time,
children always read time.

Naomi Amanda Stewart (9)
Gunthorpe School, Peterborough

Greg The Gorilla

Greg the gorilla was silly,
His arms were hairy and long.
His belly was big and fat
And his role model was King Kong.

He liked climbing the tallest trees,
And jumping the longest gaps.
He really was a daring kid
But he hated those peaked caps.

Now every year in Africa
They hold the jungle dance,
Where every single animal,
Turns up to skip and prance.

The crocodiles do the cha-cha-cha,
And the giraffes do a brilliant tango,
The gazelles do the jitterbug
But Greg eats a mango.

Then he waltzes around the floor,
Then tangos or does some ballet,
He cheers on the warthogs
Who dance the YMCA.

Nathan Giles-Donovan (11)
Henham & Ugley Primary School, Henham

Hazel The Hippo

Hazel was a grumpy hippo,
Whose body was rather fat,
Although her legs were slightly short,
She sat on a thick reed mat.

She was very good at swimming,
And lounging in mud, being lazy,
She complained and honked and snorted,
Because she was rather crazy.

Now every year in Africa,
They hold the jungle dance,
Where every single animal
Turns up to skip and prance.

The sassy snakes do the salsa,
The rough rhinos come alive,
The cheeky chimps dance the cha-cha-cha,
And the jumping jackals do the jive.

Rhiannah Whitelock (10)
Henham & Ugley Primary School, Henham

Ellie The Elephant

Ellie the elephant was big and wide,
She was covered in rough grey skin.
Although she was a handsome one,
You would never find her thin.

She was very good at running wild,
And very hard to catch,
With those big feet that she had,
She could never find a match.

Now lots of animals came at once,
To this very special dance.
Sometimes they like to waltz,
While others simply prance.

The monkeys have a swinging beat,
The lions do ballet,
Rhinos do the raunchy rumba,
And the hippos usually sway.

Rosie Greaves (11)
Henham & Ugley Primary School, Henham

Leo The Lion

Leo was a lion,
His tail was fat but long.
His paws were small and tiny,
His talent was that he was strong.

He was very good at jumping,
Leaping and dancing as well,
But when he had a secret,
He couldn't help but tell.

Now every year in Africa,
They hold the jungle dance,
Where every single animal,
Turns up to skip and prance.

The cheetahs with their rounded spots,
Danced the cha-cha-cha,
And even though they danced quite well,
Leo was the star!

Sally Reeve-Arnold (11)
Henham & Ugley Primary School, Henham

Emma The Elephant

Emma was a huge elephant
Whose trunk was long and wide,
She ran around throughout the day,
But she could never ever hide.

She was very good at smelling,
So she had a lot of fun.
Her ears kept her cool in the day
Even though she weighed a ton.

Now every year in Africa,
They hold the jungle dance,
Where every single animal,
Turns up to skip and prance.

The lions danced the jazzy jive,
The cheetahs did the cha-cha-cha.
The hyenas had a great laugh
But never took it too far.

Charlotte Albiston (10)
Henham & Ugley Primary School, Henham

Elise The Elephant

Elise was an elephant,
Whose trunk was long and thin,
She rolled in mud each morning,
But still had lovely skin.

She liked to play hide-and-seek,
And found all the good spaces.
Her friends were of the adventurous type,
Who liked to go to lots of places.

Now every year in Africa,
They hold the jungle dance,
Where every single animal,
Turned up to skip and prance.

The slithery snake did the salsa,
The worrying warthog, the waltz,
The cheeky cheetah danced the cha-cha-cha,
While the hippo had lots of faults.

Jessica Hogg (11)
Henham & Ugley Primary School, Henham

Zoe The Zebra

Zoe the zebra was a frisky girl,
She looked like a miniature horse,
Was black and white like a chalkboard,
And she never drank chocolate sauce.

She liked to be chased by lions,
With her friend who was King Kong.
When she went to visit him
She ended up seeing Ting Tong.

Now every year in Africa,
They hold the jungle dance,
Where every single animal,
Turns up to skip and prance.

The chimps did the YMCA
The lions danced in LA.
The rhinos did the cha-cha-cha,
And the gorillas did ballet!

Henry Parker (11)
Henham & Ugley Primary School, Henham

Lorna The Leopard

Lorna was a graceful leopard,
With an expensive fur coat.
Her eyes were as honest as the sky,
And her favourite meal was goat.

She loved to have a Jacuzzi,
And a manicure every day.
She lounged about her elegant home,
While she yakked to her best friend, May.

Now every year in Africa,
They hold the jungle dance,
Where every single animal,
Turns up to skip and prance.

The rhinos do the raunchy rumba,
The slithery snakes prefer the salsa.
The jackals dance the jumpy jive,
While the cheeky cheetahs cha-cha-cha.

Eloise Robinson (11)
Henham & Ugley Primary School, Henham

Misha The Meerkat

Misha was a meerkat,
Who was small, bouncy and fat.
She minced around all morning,
Got tired and sat on a mat.

Her eyes were small and beady,
Good for digging in the ground.
She had a friend called Jim Bob
And bound him round and round.

Now every year in Africa,
They hold the jungle dance,
Where every single animal,
Turned up to slip and prance.

The chimpanzees do the cha-cha-cha,
The rutting rhinos prefer the rumba.
The slimy snakes do the salsa,
But Misha just had a slumber.

Rosina Brooks (11)
Henham & Ugley Primary School, Henham

Leon The Lion

Leon was a scary lion,
With teeth so sharp and strong.
He was the fastest of the lot
And liked to hit the gong.

He was the best at catching prey,
And eating it for his lunch.
But when the birds came to view
He took the whole darn bunch.

Now every year in Africa,
They hold the jungle dance,
Where every single animal,
Turns up to skip and prance.

The hyenas do the 'ha ha ha'
And chuckle in their brunch.
The orang-utan does the tango
Whilst eating, 'Munch, munch, munch!'

Adam Machin (10)
Henham & Ugley Primary School, Henham

Clara The Cheetah

Clara was a spotty cheetah,
Who ran around all day.
She also had a very long tail,
Problem was, it always got in her way.

She was always very hungry,
And always ate her tea,
One time she went out hunting,
And bit off someone's knee.

Now every year in Africa,
They hold a jungle dance.
Where every single animal,
Turns up to skip and prance.

The snakes slithered the salsa,
The monkeys never missed the tango.
The cheetahs do the jive,
And the others ate some mangoes.

Gina Martinelli (11)
Henham & Ugley Primary School, Henham

Gordon The Gazelle

Gordon was a graceful gazelle,
Whose legs were long and thin.
But his ears were tiny and pointed,
And he had a friend called 'Lynn'.

He was very good at running,
And munching fresh green grass,
He also enjoyed a cup of tea,
Out of his thermos flask.

Now every year in Africa,
They hold the jungle dance,
Where every single animal,
Turns up to skip and prance.

The cheeky monkeys do the cha-cha-cha
The crazy hippo likes to rumba.
The giraffe attempts the salsa,
While the lion just had a slumber.

Benjamin Clark (11)
Henham & Ugley Primary School, Henham

Gary The Gorilla

Gary was a big and hairy gorilla,
He had a very fat belly.
He swung from tree to tree,
And his favourite food was jelly.

Gary was a little bit dim,
He was a very silly bloke.
He drank beer all day
Then he played a practical joke.

Now every year in Africa
They hold the jungle dance,
Where every single animal
Turns up to skip and prance.

Gary would do the waltz,
Everybody had great fun.
The crocodiles did the cha-cha,
The animals danced in the sun.

Michael Jordan (10)
Henham & Ugley Primary School, Henham

My Family

My family's crazy
They're barking, they're mad,
Half are just weird
And half are plain bad.

When adults are nearby
My sister is nice,
Near our parents, she's sugar
But really she's spice.

My brother looks like an angel,
So sweet and so cute,
On the outside a cherub,
But inside a brute.

My parents are raving,
So kind but so mad,
I think they are great,
My mum and my dad.

There is one more person,
As mad as can be.
The maddest in my family,
Has to be *me!*

Poppy Allen-Quarmby (11)
Hexton JMI School, Hitchin

A Cautionary Tale

Emma was a girl that's fat,
Plump and round, with a big green hat,
She didn't like to run around,
She'd much rather sit still on the ground.

All she would do is eat,
Although she already had fat feet.
She started to sit on the floor all day,
Instead of going out to play.

Emma's friend was thin,
But always had to win.
Whenever she was in a race,
She always had a fast pace.

Emma went to school,
But broke all the rules.
She had to stay in
And got thrown in the bin.

Then one day she ate too much food,
And this completely changed her mood.
She was so fed up with being fat,
She decided to be as skinny as a rat.

Lily Rogerson (8)
Hexton JMI School, Hitchin

Lucy Locket

There was a girl called Lucy Locket,
And yes she had a hole in her pocket.

She sucked her bright red, shiny thumb,
And then was struck completely dumb.

She was asked out on an expensive date,
And what do you think would be her fate?

She sucked her bright red, shiny thumb,
Until the teacher said, 'Why so glum?'

'It was that horrible mean old Kate Palmer,
She shoved me right over in drama!'

She sucked her bright red, shiny thumb,
When singing, they were told to hum.

They went up and down the horrible scales
And were told some heroic tales.

She sucked her bright red, shiny thumb,
Still waiting for her end to come.

Her thumb, it fell upon the floor,
The terrible thumb, finger or claw.

She never sucked her bright red thumb.

Lucy Rosser (10)
Hexton JMI School, Hitchin

John

John the exhausted boy,
Was too tired to play with his toys.
He was too tired to think,
Because he needed a drink.
When it was time to have his lunch,
All he could do was kick and punch.

Jamie Rose (8)
Hexton JMI School, Hitchin

The Stroppy Girl

There is a stroppy girl
Who lives just down my road
And if she doesn't get what she wants
Then she will overload.

'I want this!
I want that!'

One day she cried, 'Give me some chocolate,'
About two hours before lunch,
She even kept on stuffing her face
Until the next day's brunch.

'I want this!
I want that!'

In the end her parents got so mad,
They shouted at the girl and made her very sad,
And in the end she said, 'It really wasn't me Dad.'
But he replied, *'Be quiet!* You silly little cad!'

Jamie White (10)
Hexton JMI School, Hitchin

A Cautionary Tale

Ben is a boy who always burps,
Because of his meals, he often slurps.
He burps when he is at school,
That's against the rule.
He burped in the school garden,
But never said, 'Pardon!'
So he was called to the Head
As the teacher saw red.
'Ben you are so rude,
You'd better change your attitude.
Your manners you must mend
Or the girlies you'll offend.'

Max Wolstencroft (8)
Hexton JMI School, Hitchin

John Awake!

John the exhausted boy,
Was too tired to play with his toys,
On the day Dad went away
He fell asleep
And missed his mother weep.

John the exhausted boy
Was too tired to play with his toys.
Got up to have his lunch,
And on an apple did munch.
Noticed his mother was crying,
And his dad had gone flying.

John the exhausted boy,
Was too tired to play with his toys.
He took a nap,
While Mum found a map,
To join his dad
Because she was sad.

Prian Chauhan (10)
Hexton JMI School, Hitchin

Billy Silly And His Nails

Billy Silly bites his nails,
He even eats the garden snails.
His sister really was a scream,
And she lived in a total dream.
One day, as on she gazed,
Lost in some unconscious haze.
She saw him open up his mouth
Pile snails in from north and south.
She let out an enormous wail,
As brother Billy left a trail
Of slime upon the ground
Where he'd eaten the snails, that he'd found.

Annabel Katie Forde (11)
Hexton JMI School, Hitchin

Jamie And Amy

There was a boy called Jamie,
He had a little sister called Amy.

She went in the garden,
He heard her say pardon,
As she was eating a snail.
He went very pale,
He dragged her in
And put her in the garbage bin.

The mother rescued her, by catching her hair,
And hanging onto the clothes that she did wear.
She decided to ask her daughter;
'Shall we send him off for slaughter?'
'No mum, just send him to his room
I don't want to see his doom.'
Then the brother said, 'I'm very sorry!'
So she got him a toy lorry.

Ben Lawson (10)
Hexton JMI School, Hitchin

A Cautionary Tale

Susan was a greedy child,
Her behaviour was very wild.
Before her mum had set the table
She had eaten all she was able.

Susan had lots of woes
And she quickly grows,
One day her mum asked her to come,
And she said she looked like a plum.

Susan ate so much she became ill,
Hoping the doctor would find her a new pill.
But when he saw her, he was full of dread,
And said, 'If you don't stop eating, you'll soon be dead!'

Abigail Gee (8)
Hexton JMI School, Hitchin

A Cautionary Tale

There was a cat, who was very fat,
She was black and her name was Pat.
I will tell you her tragic end;
(So your habits you may mend).

Tom the young lad sat on a chair,
Unaware it was Pat's lair.
The cat suffered a squashing,
As flat as the crinkled washing.

Poor Pat who was very fat
Is now very flat,
But Tom's bum has turned into a
Giant plum!

Amy Rogerson (9)
Hexton JMI School, Hitchin

Behind The Gate

In the garden there's a little gate,
The garden is owned by a girl called Kate,
She has long hair, she has a good heart,
She likes to drive in her little go-kart.

Little Kate's always wondered what's behind the gate
And on the other side Emma wonders about her fate,
They both think there's two gates,
They also wish they had mates.

Little Kate walked out of her house,
Turned the handle that squeaked like a mouse.
Little Kate saw a building made of cream,
Made a charge for her fantastic dream.

Stuart Hall (8)
Holbrook Primary School, Holbrook

Rugby Cup Final - England V Wales 2003

Kick-off is at half-past three,
TVs go on out at sea.
England stroll out onto the pitch,
The crowd go wild as if controlled by a switch.

Wales walk on, wanting their share of attention,
But the crowd grow silent, full of tension.
Wilkinson kicks. Wow, watch it go!
Woodward gets hit in the head, sitting in the front row.

Dillalio tackles, forward pass, scrum!
Josh Lucy's just broken his thumb.
Scrum is broken by Steven Jones and he's got the ball,
Intercepted by Matt Dawson. Ouch! What a fall.

England make a break through
Welsh fans hiss and boo.
Lucy, Dillalio, Ben Kay,
Jason Robinson kicks, but the ball goes astray.

England adjust and go for a try,
Williams misses a tackle and falls on his thigh.
Keep it up England, almost there,
Five-nil to England and Wales stop and stare.

Whistle goes and the crowd goes wild,
People take off their tops, even though it's barely mild.
Final score 5-0 to England
But they've got to go and prepare to play Finland.

Sean Cuddihy (9)
Holbrook Primary School, Holbrook

The Vehicle

We're going on a plane.
Oh no! We're in a shower of rain.
There's a little boy, he's insane.
We're going on a plane.

We're going in a car.
It's not very far.
We're going to play golf, I'll get a par.
We're going in a car.

We're going on a train.
Luckily there is no rain.
There's a lady with a broken leg.
I think she's in pain.
We're going on a train.

We're going on a bike.
Going to meet my friend Mike.
He says we're fishing for pike.
We're going on a bike.

We're going to the end the day
In a happy way.
There's a knock on the door, cool, Uncle Ray!
We're going to end the day.

Taylor Handel (8)
Holbrook Primary School, Holbrook

Spring

Singing birds in the trees,
Pansies dancing in the beds.
Ringing bells from the church,
In the nests there are eggs.

Near the trees, badgers feed,
Here and there go swallows.
Flowers grow everywhere,
Everyone picks the weeds.

Harriet Sawyer (9)
Holbrook Primary School, Holbrook

The Big Fat Bear

You can't beware of the big fat bear.
He might just tickle you under there.

And if you are really bad
You'll see him get cross and mad.

But if you have been really good,
He'll take you to tea in his wood.

When it comes to saying goodnight,
He'll share his bed and turn off the light.

Oliver Sellers (9)
Holbrook Primary School, Holbrook

I Like Things

I like flowers because they have powers,
I see lovely big red roses,
People smell them with their noses.
I like bikes, the best is mine,
My bike is big and it shines.
I like my PlayStation 2 because it is fun,
I shoot with a big, strong gun.

Jordan Goodwin (9)
Holbrook Primary School, Holbrook

The Bright Digger

A digger is as yellow as the sun,
It sounds very loud, when it starts to run.

It lives in the dump,
Has lots of stuff to lump.

The digger gets smaller as it goes away,
It doesn't want to go, it wants to stay.

Samuel Kocurek (8)
Holbrook Primary School, Holbrook

Cross-Country

Whistles blowing, wind dashing,
People rushing.
Kicking, falling, flags blowing,
People cheating.
Past the school, past the trees,
Into the forest they go.

The people in the crowd,
Cheering noisily and loud.
They don't know when
They are going to stop.
The winner comes into sight,
Rushes as hard as he can.
Through the tape.
Phew! It's over.

Joshua Allday (8)
Holbrook Primary School, Holbrook

Nonsense

I jumped out of my pyjamas
And took off my bed,
I fell up the stairs
And roasted my spread.
I pogo-sticked to school,
Our class went on a trip,
It hurt a lot.
At the end of the day,
I flopped into my light
And turned out my bed,
Gooday, I mean goodnight.

Paddy Atkinson (9)
Holbrook Primary School, Holbrook

Mr Boggapilla

Mr Boggapilla got himself into a situation,
That was much more of a complication,
So he had a big conversation,
He wanted to go on a vacation.

Mr Boggapilla had an operation,
He lost all sense of communication.
He bought a brochure containing information,
He watched a film made from animation.

He went back to school for some education,
His friends said he had a naughty reputation.
His teacher exclaimed, 'What a strange creation.'
Every time he went to the loo, he had constipation.

George Rennison (8)
Holbrook Primary School, Holbrook

A Little Bear

At the bottom of the garden, lives a little bear,
Usually you can find him, eating a pear.
He is all fluffy and so cute,
He wears a suit and plays the flute.
He has such a dark brown coat.

He looks just like a fluffy goat,
He does not have a care.
He is my best bear,
I love to take him everywhere.

Nicole Anscomb (9)
Holbrook Primary School, Holbrook

My Dog

My dog sounds like a walrus
He is as brown as a Malteser
And as white as a McFlurry
He loves ice cream
And goes slow until the gate opens.

He loves to sleep with his toys
And catches tennis balls
He likes to chase me and
He loves the sun
But he doesn't like the snow
He loves to watch the Suffolk Show.

He likes to watch my dad play football,
He jumps up at people,
He gets sleepy easily
He loves me and
He likes bees.

Brooke Ward-Ashton (9)
Holbrook Primary School, Holbrook

My Cat

Milo is my tomcat
Who usually sits on his mat.
Milo has got ginger fur
Reminds me of the colour of myrrh.
Milo is a happy cat
And when he has food, he becomes fat.
Milo likes to jump on my bed,
When he thinks it's time to be fed.

Eleanor Carey (8)
Holbrook Primary School, Holbrook

Seasons

In spring the world is full of corn
And all the baby lambs are born.

In summer the world is hot,
With all the wasps swarming around the pot.

In autumn the leaves start to fall
And all the cars begin to stall.

In winter the world is cold and bare,
Now it needs some summer care.

The seasons always change, from hot to cold,
And people grow from young to old.

Phoebe Maunder (9)
Holbrook Primary School, Holbrook

Water

There was a ship that was red in the sea
It sailed by and picked up me.

I saw a fin, it was a shark
Crikey! I was lucky, it wasn't dark.

The people on the ship did scream
When they awoke from their dream.

They were thinking of going swimming
As the cold blue water was brimming.

Declan Lee (8)
Holbrook Primary School, Holbrook